COMPARATIVE SOCIAL ASSISTANCE

Studies in Cash and Care

Editors: Sally Baldwin and Jonathan Bradshaw

Cash benefits and care services together make a fundamental contribution to human welfare. After income derived from work, they are arguably the most important determinants of living standards. Indeed, many households are almost entirely dependent on benefits and services which are socially provided. Moreover, welfare benefits and services consume the lion's share of public expenditure. The operation, impact and interaction of benefits and services is thus an important focus of research on social policy.

Policy related work in this field tends to be disseminated to small specialist audiences in the form of mimeographed research reports or working papers and perhaps later published, more briefly, in journal articles. In consequence public debate about vital social issues is sadly ill-informed. This series is designed to fill this gap by making the details of important empirically-based research more widely available.

Comparative Social Assistance

Localisation and Discretion

JOHN DITCH
JONATHAN BRADSHAW
JOCHEN CLASEN
MEG HUBY
MARGARET MOODIE

Ashgate

Aldershot • Brookfield USA • Singapore • Sydney

Published by
Ashgate Publishing Ltd
Gower House
Croft Road
Aldershot
Hants GU11 3HR
England

Ashgate Publishing Company
Old Post Road
Brookfield
Vermont 05036
USA

British Library Cataloguing in Publication Data
Comparative social assistance : localisation and
    discretion. - (Cash & care)
    1. Public welfare - Europe
    I. Ditch, John
    361.9'4

Library of Congress Catalog Card Number: 97-77553

ISBN 1 84014 346 0

Printed and bound by Athenaeum Press, Ltd.,
Gateshead, Tyne & Wear.

Contents

Acknowledgements

A study of this kind, conducted in such a short time frame, can only come close to success due to the goodwill of colleagues and informants in four countries. The following people have all contributed to the study and we are grateful to them.

In Germany, Berthold Dietz of Münster; Dr Helmut Hartmann, State Social Office, Hamburg; Mr Wolf D. Klatt, Social Welfare Office, Bremen; Dr Lutz Leisering, Bremen University; Dr Johannes Steffen, Arbeiterkammer Bremen; Dr Manfred Wienand, Dr Imlau-Staupendahl and Mr Höft-Dzemski, German Association for Public and Private Welfare, Frankfurt.

In the Netherlands, Mr Crouwell, VNG; Ed Theunen, Sociale Dienst; Jan Voss, KPMG Management Consulting, The Hague; Dr Wim Van Oorschot, Tilburg University; Sylvia Korevaar, LVO (National Organisation for Change); Tanja Merkolbach, Ministerie van Sociale Zaken en Werkgelgenheid.

In Sweden, Eva Bergstrom, Professor Karin Tengvald, Pira Milton of the National Board of Health and Welfare, and Johanes Wiklund, of the Stockholm County Administrative Board. Marten Lagergren of the Ministry of Health and Social Affairs and Magdalena Brasch from the Ministry of Finance. Leif Klingensjo of the Swedish Association of Local Authorities. Harriet Westerlund, Christina Enoksson and Zara Ghaffari from Solna. Tommy Lundberg, Pia Gunnarson and Joanna Tiderman from Strangnas. Joachim Palme of the Swedish Institute for Social Research and a Special Advisor to the Minister of Social Affairs and Ake Bergmark in the Department of Social Work at the University of Stockholm.

In Switzerland, Professor F. Höepflinger (University of Zürich), M.G. Piotet (Dept. of Health and Social Affairs, Canton of Vand), M.K. Ferroni (Swiss Conference of Institutions for Social Assistance, and Canton of Graubünden), M.E. Zürcher (Sec. General of Conference of the Cantons' Heads for Social Affairs), M.H. Maurer (Canton of Geneva), M.K. Jaggi (Canton of Berne), M.M.

Hohn (City of Berne) and M.W. Schmid (City of Zürich), M.C. Malherbe, Federal Office for Social Insurance.

Dr Helen Bolderson and Dr Deborah Mabbett, Brunel University provided information on their research into the delivery of benefits. Emma Carmel of the University of York undertook a review of literature on the dynamics of centre-local relations. We are also grateful to Owen Thorpe, Helen Gadd, Kay Pattison and Julia Chilvers of the DSS for most helpful comments on earlier drafts of this report.

This report is based on research commissioned by the Department of Social Security (United Kingdom). Responsibility for the report, its contents and conclusions, rests with the authors alone.

We are grateful to Rebecca Harrison of the Department of Social Policy and Social Work at the University of York for typesetting the manuscript.

1 Introduction

The Department of Social Security received the final reports from a major study of Social Assistance arrangements in the 24 OECD countries in October 1995 (Eardley et al, 1996). Although this research was comprehensive a number of important questions remained to be investigated in more detail. Specifically there is interest in the policy context, organisational structures and procedures, strengths and weaknesses of Social Assistance systems in those countries where a degree of sub-national variation exists in respect of policy, financing, administration or application of discretion. A further study was commissioned (November 1995) to examine the strengths and weaknesses of these arrangements in four European countries: Germany, the Netherlands, Sweden and Switzerland. This is the report of that review.

The objectives for the study were agreed as being to:

1. Assess, according to agreed criteria, how local control of Social Assistance schemes works in practice.

2. Examine the relationship between central, regional and local authorities in the financing and administration of Social Assistance.

3. Identify financial and political pressure points and emerging policy options.

These objectives were subsequently elaborated, following discussion between the research team and policy customers, to specify a list of criteria around which more detailed questions have been formulated. The criteria and questions (presented in full in Appendix A) related to the following dimensions: the contexts within which Social Assistance developed and is required to function; the structure of centre-local relations: financial responsibility; the sensitivity of Social Assistance to the circumstances of recipients and the dynamics of local economies; the extent of peer pressure and the control of fraud; the strengths and weaknesses of Social Assistance schemes and policy options for change.

Methods

The following methods have been used to address these questions:

1.   Re-examination of data submitted by officials and experts as part of the previous study of Social Assistance (Eardley et al, 1996).

2.   A meeting between the research team, policy customers and DSS research staff at which evaluative criteria and detailed research questions were identified. (See Appendix A.)

3.   Preparation of questionnaires which were sent to officials and experts in each of the four countries. The questionnaires presented the questions which are outlined in Appendix A.

4.   Observations of Social Assistance schemes in operation and personal interviews with officials and experts in each of the countries. (See acknowledgements for names and institutional affiliations.)

5.   A review of recent research reports and literature.

The timescale for the study, from commission in early November to draft final report in mid-January, required that the research was conducted expeditiously. Respondents, from each of the countries, were required to prepare statements on the operation of the Social Assistance schemes and to provide answers to specific questions. The respondents also arranged for observational visits and face to face interviews; on the basis of their responses (both written and oral) the following report has been prepared.

2 Social Assistance and centre-local relations

Schemes of Social Assistance are available in almost all countries, where they seek to make statutory provision to meet the needs of residents or citizens. However, the scope of these arrangements, their coverage and diversity, their value to recipients and their interaction with other parts of social security systems and structures of governance have received little systematic attention. There are no internationally agreed or consistent definitions of Social Assistance and responsibility for policy, financing and delivery can be held by either national, regional or local authorities; indeed, in some countries, there is a significant role for non-governmental organisations.

This chapter provides a double context (social security and governance structures) within which it is possible to describe and evaluate the structure, strengths and weaknesses of Social Assistance. First, the status and role of means and asset tested benefits in relation to insurance and categorical benefits is described. This, in turn, leads to a disaggregation of the key types of Social Assistance benefit and the elaboration criteria used to create regimes which have certain aspects of structure and effectiveness in common. Each of the four countries in the study is assigned to a different regime, however there is a common thread running between the Social Assistance schemes in each of the four countries: they all, more-or-less, have structures and delivery systems which operate at a sub-national level. The structures of governance, and the traditional emphasis on federalism, decentralisation and subsidiarity are the subject of the second context discussed in this chapter. Arrangements for the financing and administration of social security, and of Social Assistance in particular, cannot be understood other than against the background of constitutional provision and political practices in each country.

Although all countries are experiencing similar demographic and economic pressures, options for the reform of Social Assistance reflect the diverse political structures and values of each state. Policies and delivery structures are particular to a national context: what works in one context may not work in another.

In this chapter, Social Assistance will also be placed within a wider context of the methods by which statutory authorities can allocate resources, either in cash or kind, to individuals or households. Two channels other than Social Assistance are available: first, there are universal or categorical benefits, which are related neither to income nor employment status, but made available to citizens who fall within prescribed social categories, such as being a mother with a dependent child or children. The second category include the full range of social insurance benefits which are related to both employment status and contributions record. Social Assistance benefits, the third channel, are related to neither category nor contributions, but are income or asset tested. However, within this broad definition there are three distinctive types of Social Assistance.(See Table 2.1) First, all countries within the OECD (with the exception of Greece and Portugal) have **general assistance** schemes which provide cash assistance for all (or virtually all) people falling below a specified minimum income standard. Such schemes include Income Support in the United Kingdom and Minimex in Belgium. Second, there are **categorical Social Assistance** schemes which provide assistance for specified groups. In the UK such benefits include Family Credit and Disability Working Allowance; in Germany and the Netherlands it includes unemployment assistance. Finally, there is **tied assistance** which may provide either cash, goods or services to those defined as being in need. Because housing costs can represent such a large proportion of individual or household expenditure, support for housing can be a large component of Social Assistance. Housing benefits therefore make up a dominant part of tied assistance with other benefits taking account of local taxes (Council Tax Benefit in the UK), free school meals or Medicaid (in the USA).

For the four countries included in this study the following taxonomy applies:

Table 2.1   Social Assistance Benefits

Country	General Assistance	Categorical Assistance	Housing Assistance	Other tied Assistance
Germany	Sozialhilfe: subsistence aid	Arbeitslosenhilfe	Wohngeld	Sozialhilfe: aid in special circumstances
Netherlands	Algemene Bijstand (ABW)	Regulation for Unemployed Employees (RWW); Income Provisions for Older and Partially Disabled Workers (IOAW), Income Provisions for Formerly Self-Employed (IOAZ), Supplementary Benefit (TW)	Housing Benefit	
Sweden	Social Assistance			
Switzerland	Aide Sociale/Soziale Fursorge	Supplementary retirement and invalidity pension		

In the previous study (Eardley, et al 1996) the Social Assistance systems of the OECD countries were grouped into 7 categories, each of which emphasised characteristics held in common (ibid. pp.244-246). The frameworks were indicative and schematic but were a useful way of aligning common characteristics. However they took account of dominant factors, and in particular the following dimensions:

- extent, cost and coverage of Social Assistance
- extent to which schemes are general or categorical
- relative value of benefits
- extent of local dimension in financing, regulation and administration
- operation of means test
- extent of officials' discretion

It should be noted that the resulting categories no more imply that countries within a given category are similar in every respect than they imply that countries assigned to different categories have nothing in common. Germany, the Netherlands, Sweden and Switzerland are cases in point. They were assigned to different regimes:

Table 2.2   Four countries as examples

Country	Regime
Germany	**welfare state with integrated safety net**. A strong, widespread, Social Assistance structure with strongly entrenched rights and average generosity.
Netherlands	**dual Social Assistance**. Originally providing categorical Social Assistance but now developing a general basic safety net.
Sweden	**residual Social Assistance**. Historical experience of full-employment and generous social insurance benefits has tended to displace the significance of Social Assistance. A strict means test and traditions of family obligation.
Switzerland	**highly decentralised Social Assistance with local discretion**. Highly localised, extensive use of officer discretion, generous benefits closely linked to social work practice and small numbers of claimants.

Source: Derived from Eardley et al (1996), pp.168-171.

Despite being assigned to different models, as already noted, each of these countries shares a dimension in common: to a greater or lesser extent they operate within a framework which allows for sub-national variation in respect of, policy, financing or the delivery of Social Assistance. Before considering the operation of each scheme separately and in some detail, it is necessary to briefly elaborate some of the key dimensions of centre-local relations within the framework of studies of European governance and public policy. Such a review seeks to distinguish between forms and levels of governance and to explain significant differences between key terms.

Forms of devolution: federalism, deconcentration and decentralisation

Constitutional principles, political structures and the day-to-day dynamics of centre-local relations all impact on the extent to which responsibility for the development of policy, the financing of schemes and the delivery of benefits is devolved to sub-national authorities. Of the four countries in the study, Switzerland is a federal state with a relatively weak centre and Germany is a federal state with a strong centre; the Netherlands is a decentralised unitary state, composed of seven provinces which are declining in political significance; Sweden is a unitary state with a strong tradition of local government.

Federalism is a form of constitutional and political arrangement whereby the governance of a country is divided between a central (federal) authority and smaller, relatively autonomous, political authorities. Each of the smaller authorities is legally independent in respect of a range of policy areas. In Switzerland, a federal state par excellence, the cantons are responsible for policy, finance and delivery of Social Assistance. In this context the relationship between federal (national) authority and individual cantons is mediated by a formal separation of powers, in a way which is coordinated and balanced rather than hierarchical or top-down.

In Germany, which also has a federal structure and constitution, the Länder have significantly less independence/autonomy and are subject to controlling mechanisms more akin to those used to control local governments in unitary states.

Table 2.3   Governance and Social Assistance

Country	Form	Type
Germany	Federal	Decentralised
Netherlands	Unitary	Decentralised
Sweden	Unitary	Deconcentrated
Switzerland	Federal	Deconcentrated

In addition to the differences between the countries which exist as a result of history and national political culture, it is necessary to distinguish, at a theoretical level, between **political deconcentration** on the one hand, and **administrative/executive decentralisation** on the other. The former is concerned to facilitate access to the political process at a regional or local level; special needs can be articulated, politicians can be held accountable and policies or services adapted to prevailing circumstances. The latter is less concerned with policies than administration: subordinate authorities (more accurately, agencies) are responsible for the implementation of policy and the delivery of service. Budgets can be devolved, targets and performance measures can be introduced and the service can be brought closer to its recipients or customers. Such an approach is consistent with general tendencies across Europe to break up large, centralised, bureaucracies without relinquishing central control over policy making.

Trends in centre-local relations

Throughout Europe relationships between national governments and subordinate/local authorities are subject to review and revision. Hollis *et.al* (1994) have identified six factors which are impacting upon and shape centre-local relations. They are:

-    a re-examination of the role of the public sector, including the responsibilities of state structure to provide rather than facilitate or regulate service provision.

- a renewed interest in the practice of subsidiarity whereby no decisions are to be taken at a higher level of political authority than is necessary to implement the decision effectively.

- a growth in regionalism reflected in political and cultural activities across the continent of Europe.

- a commitment to effective accountability procedures.

- an expansion of the role and responsibilities of the private sector.

- an expansion of the role and responsibilities of the voluntary sector.

In Germany, the Netherlands and Sweden there has been, for the past five years or so, consistent emphasis on decentralisation and enhancing the role of the lowest tier of administration. In the Netherlands the establishment of regions is leading to the decline of the historically dominant provincial tier of local government. However, this trend is not cost free. As Hollis *et al* argue:

...there is often a conflict between the need for localness on the one hand and cost-effectiveness on the other. Some countries have tried to solve this by multi-tiered systems, where larger services are provided by the higher tier authorities. In other words, it is common for small local authorities to combine to provide major services either directly or by contract. However, there is no systematic evidence available to suggest that localness generates more participation in local government or satisfaction with local services and the local democratic process. (Hollis, *et al*, 1994, p.10)

All across Europe there have been severe restrictions on local authority spending and this results in the need to rank policy priorities and to attain greater cost effectiveness. Ironically, central governments are placing greater emphasis on both decentralisation and subsidiarity and this leads to greater powers and responsibilities for local authorities: this in turn leads to greater financial pressure on the local authorities. In consequence, two responses are adopted: first, there are widespread pressures to reduce bureaucracy and for local authorities to move from providing to facilitating and regulating service; second, local authorities will resist the allocation of new responsibilities unless they are accompanied by matching funds. In addition there is a quest for greater variety and new forms of funding and this involves more emphasis on user charges and collaboration with private and not for profit sectors.

Conclusion

Despite considerable variation in the structures, systems and conventions of governance in the four countries (see Table 2.3) there is a notable similarity in the problems and challenges they face. The implications of economic change and recession are placing higher demands on public institutions at a time when financial resources are most stretched. In consequence each country is placing additional emphasis on the need for diversification (involving private and not-for-profit sectors) and new forms of decentralisation. However, there is a contradiction between trends towards executive localisation (decentralisation which creates opportunities for cost-effectiveness and responsiveness to local circumstances) and the prevailing resource constraint which narrows capacity to apply discretion in a positive way at local level.

3 Germany

Introduction

Germany is the largest country in the European Union and has recently undergone profound political, administrative and economic change as a result of the re-integration of former East Germany into the Federal Republic. Political structures were established in 1949 when the Basic Law *(Grundgesetz*, the German Constitution) was confirmed. There is a four tier structure of government: a federal government and three tiers of sub-national authority. Originally there were over 30,000 *Gemeinden* (communities) but a process of rationalization has reduced these to approximately 16,000 in 1992. The following table presents a summary of data on the structure of local government.

Table 3.1   Number of authorities by tier of Government

Tier	Number	Population Range
Level 1 (national)	1	81.3m
Level 2 (Länder)	13	1m - 17.3m
	3 (cities)	0.68m; 1.6m; 3.4m
Level 3 (Landkreise)	416	31,000-650,000
Level 3 (Stadkreise) - Kreisefreie Städte	117	35,000-1,260,000
Level 4 (Gemeinden)	16,043	<500 - 5,401 >500,000 - 13

Source: Hollis et al, 1994, p. 69.

The States *(Länder)* have their own elected parliaments, governments and departments. They have influence at the national level through representation in the second chamber *(Bundesrat)*. Between states and communes *(Gemeinden)* are a variety of intermediate structures: *Kreise* (counties), *Stadtkreise* (county boroughs) and *Kreisefreie Städte* (large cities). In the former East Germany there has been considerable re-organisation and investment in new structures: this process continues.

With a population in excess of 81 million, Germany has one of the lowest fertility rates in the OECD and one of the highest rates of immigration. It has the third highest proportion of lone parents and is challenged by the effects and implications of a rapidly ageing population resulting in a high dependency ratio. Unemployment has increased significantly during the 1990s but remains below the average for both the EU and the OECD.

These changes have impacted on both the structure and financing of social protection. Whereas between 1980 and 1991 total expenditure on social protection expressed as a per cent of GDP decreased from 28.7 per cent to 26.6 per cent, total Social Assistance expenditure expressed as a proportion of social security increased from 7 per cent to 12 per cent: an increase of 167 per cent. In 1992, 6.8 per cent of Germany's population were in receipt of Social Assistance, an increase of 172 per cent over the previous decade (Eardley et al, 1996).

Germany's overall social security system is quintessentially derived from the corporatist and Bismarckian tradition of social insurance, which has historically aimed to replace earnings in the event of illness, disability and in old age, at a level closely related to previous income when in work (Clasen & Freeman, 1994). There are three main branches: the first provides cover against the most common social risks including old age, unemployment, invalidity, maternity and death. Entitlement is mostly based on contributions but there are some non-contributory benefits for certain categories of public employee. The second branch provides non-contributory benefits in circumstances which imply a public liability such as war injuries or crime. The third branch includes 'assistance where need arises, or social promotion in order to guarantee equal opportunities for individual development' (see Clasen & Freeman, 1994). These include non-contributory but partially means-tested child benefits and the main Social Assistance benefit: *Sozialhilfe*.

With unification, social security arrangements of the old West Germany were extended to the East. There were some transitional arrangements. For example, the former East had no network of functioning local authority administration (or finance) to pay out Social Assistance benefits. In consequence, and contrary to West German arrangements, the unemployed and other claimants were credited as being entitled to a minimum level of insurance benefits -

irrespective of former earnings levels. In this way, claimants in the New Länder were kept within the social insurance 'net' rather than having recourse to *Sozialhilfe*.

As the social security system, and Social Assistance structures in particular, have been developed in the former East these transitional arrangements have come to an end. The only remaining difference relates to the slightly lower benefit rates in the East, which are justified by lower living costs.

Social Assistance

The policy aims for Social Assistance (*Sozialhilfe*) in Germany derive from the Basic Law (which requires a uniformity of 'life chances' throughout the country) and seek to enable recipients to 'lead a life in human dignity'. As the 'last safety net' within the German social security system, it is entirely tax financed and intended to support people for only transitory and exceptional periods of life rather than to cover 'standard risks' which are supposed to be met by insurance and other types of benefits. It is guided by principles of 'need' (means-testing applies), 'individuality' (personal circumstances determine the level and elements of support for each applicant individually) and horizontal 'subsidiarity' (all other types of income, transfers and savings have to be exhausted before *Sozialhilfe* sets in). Another condition for *Sozialhilfe* is that recipients have to contribute 'according to their abilities'. For example, unemployed recipients have to be available for and willing to take up employment or labour market measures. An important objective for *Sozialhilfe*, underlying its supposedly transitory nature, is the idea that recipients should be enabled to become independent of *Sozialhilfe* receipt.

There are different types of support within the *Sozialhilfe* scheme, all of which are dependent on the existence and assessment of 'need'. The main components of *Sozialhilfe* are:

- standard benefits (*Regelsätze*) for each member of the family plus possible supplements and the cost of accommodation;
- one-off payments (*einmalige Beihilfen*) which cover items which are not required on a monthly basis (eg clothing, shoes, renovations of accommodation, furniture).

These types of support comprise the HLU (*Hilfe zum Lebensunterhalt* - subsistence benefit), which this chapter concentrates on. The other type of *Sozialhilfe* is the so-called HBL (*Hilfe in besonderen Lebenslagen* - aid in special life situations) which provides support for particular claimant groups (eg people in need of care, blind people, people with disabilities).

Sozialhilfe is regulated by the German Constitution/Basic Law, the Federal *Sozialhilfe* Act (BSHG) and the Social Code. The latter contains major principles for legal rights to public support while the BSHG is the basic legal framework for principles, benefits and organisation of Social Assistance. Legislative power for the BSHG lies with the federal government (and in particular the Ministry of Health) stipulating the legal framework as far as principles, benefits and organisation are concerned. However, *Sozialhilfe* is organised at the local and regional (*Land*) level because that is the only level at which policy aims concerning individualisation and subsidiarity can be realised. *Länder* can, for example, stipulate increases in standard benefit levels (unless the government has 'capped' the increase - which is the case in early 1996). They also issue Acts concerning the implementation of the BSHG (*Ausführungsgesetze*) and regulate questions of organisation, accountability and finance. Local communities (regional districts and the independent cities of Hamburg, Bremen and Berlin) are responsible for the administration of the BSHG, its interpretation and implementation as well as for the bulk of the funding. In short, the government legislates *Sozialhilfe*, the *Länder* communicate with each other and fix benefit levels and local authorities implement and finance the scheme.

Levels of Sozialhilfe

Except for Bavaria, the standard rates (Regelsätze) vary only very little between the old Länder. In July 1996 the monthly benefit levels in nine out of eleven Länder in the territory of the old West Germany were:

Table 3.2   Monthly Benefit Levels (actual rates)

	DM per month
Head of household	531
Child up to 7 years	266
Child up to 7 years living with lone parent	292
Child between 8 and 14	345
Child between 15 and 18	478
Older household members	425

For the New *Länder* (former East Germany) it is necessary to deduct between DM10-25 per month from these standard rates.

The standard rates are meant to cover the costs of eating; cooking; purchase and maintenance of clothing; hygiene; purchase of small household items; small repairs, lighting, electrical equipment, washing and other items of daily life such as newspapers. In addition, claimants receive the costs of accommodation; one-off payments (equal to approximately 15 per cent of standard benefit per month); supplements (normally between 20 per cent and 40 per cent of standard benefit per month) are also paid for certain groups such as those over 65 years, pregnant mothers and the disabled.

However, a 'wage rule' formally exists which requires that the total level of *Sozialhilfe* for a family has to be at least 15 per cent below the net income of an equivalent family with one earner on low wages. The rule is frequently ignored.

Finance and Control

The funding of Sozialhilfe is almost entirely the responsibility of local authorities who cover, on average, about 80 per cent of the costs and Länder who cover about 20 per cent of the costs, with variations between *Länder* stipulated by Land governments. The federal level (*Bund*) pays less than 1 per cent, for example for German *Sozialhilfe* recipients abroad.

The degree of influence between the four levels of government is largely top-down. However, by fixing levels of *Sozialhilfe* benefit and issuing implementation guidelines *Länder* have some power. Politically, they can influence government legislation via the Upper House (*Bundesrat*) which is constituted by Land governments and the Mediation Committee (composed of members of both houses), which mediates between the two Houses of Parliament whenever certain types of government legislation (basically those which affect *Länder* financially) need to be agreed upon by the Upper House. Local authorities can try to influence *Länder* via administrative channels and the government politically via umbrella organisations such as the German *Städtetag* (Association of larger cities).

Sozialhilfe is entirely tax funded. Within Germany, the bulk of tax revenue is raised centrally but shared out between the Bund, *Länder* and local authorities according to the type of tax. The Basic Law (GG §106) deals with the apportionment of taxes and is the basis for vertical tax revenue distribution. Additionally, there are mechanisms of fiscal equalisation both between *Bund* and *Länder*, among *Länder* and between local authorities within a single *Land*. These adjustments to the allocation of tax revenue are based on the principle that tax revenues should go to the regions where they were collected, while at the same time aiming to prevent an inequitable distribution of revenue between regions with different tax raising ability. The rationale for the latter is to contribute to a convergence of living standards between regions.

Different levels of governments raise revenue from some type of taxes to which they have exclusive access. For example, the federal government receives proceeds from taxes on mineral oils, *Länder* levy taxes on motor vehicles and property while the trade tax (*Gewerbesteuer*) is an important source of revenue for local authorities who also levy taxes on land and buildings. However, overall revenue from these types of exclusive taxes is relatively small compared with that from joint taxes (income tax and turnover tax), amounting to about two thirds of general tax receipt.

It is these exclusive and joint types of taxes, supplemented by fees and charges levied on local services, which constitute the budget for local authorities and therefore the basis for local authority expenditure, including *Sozialhilfe*. As with other types of expenditure, plans for *Sozialhilfe* spending for the forthcoming budget year rely on estimates and predictions and the required sum is allocated based on a number of planning procedures, fiscal considerations and past experience in order that local authorities cannot 'run out' of money for *Sozialhilfe*.

If actual expenditure for *Sozialhilfe* exceeds the sum allocated, resources may be made available via a supplementary budget if the local parliament so decides. Alternatively, local authorities may borrow in financial markets (up to a certain limit) or try to increase receipts from local services in a number of ways. Finally, expenditure on local services (eg swimming pools, theatres, kindergartens, community centres) might be cut back as well as those aspects of Social Assistance which are not required by law. The latter option has been adopted by many local authorities recently who found themselves confronted by ever increasing *Sozialhilfe* expenditure due to the impact of high and long-term unemployment in particular (but also other social changes) which has not been dealt with adequately by social insurance and other federal policies.

Sozialhilfe goes beyond monetary transfers for many recipients by including services such as debt advice, job creation schemes etc. It is therefore difficult to work out the costs of *Sozialhilfe* administration (for personnel and overheads). More importantly, the traditional way of calculating public finance expenditure in Germany means that this type of information is not available. However, public administration is currently being reformed and 'modernised': this includes the establishment of cost centres which will make the system more transparent across sectors and allow for more precise calculations of administrative costs for specific areas.

A number of checks and controls of *Sozialhilfe* expenditure exist. The administration of benefits which are legally defined are checked internally by welfare offices themselves, assessing the correct application of fiscal principles such as the suitability, legality and assessment of means. Special officers at local authority level can request samples of files. Control reports are fed back to the section heads at *Sozialhilfe* offices. Administrative guidelines issued at *Land* level constitute another check on behaviour of welfare officers. In certain *Länder* with only one tier of government (such as Bremen and Hamburg) the State Audit Office (*Landesrechnungshof*) also checks over certain areas of *Land* administration - which can include sections of the *Sozialhilfe* administration.

Coverage

In principle, all persons who reside on German territory (irrespective of age or nationality) have a right to *Sozialhilfe* if they are in need and if their income from work and other sources, including other social security transfers, assets and claims on relatives, are below a certain level depending on the applicant. It is thus a uniform scheme which is not targeted at specific groups in society. It is aimed at helping recipients to become independent of it. However, contrary to this intention *Sozialhilfe* has in fact developed into a permanent support scheme for certain groups in society such as many unemployed, many lone parents and many foreign residents.

In 1993 new legislation was introduced which effectively transferred responsibility for the support of asylum seekers from the BSHG to a new Law (*Asylbewerberleistungsgesetz*) which now regulates benefits for this group in their first year of residence in Germany. Support granted within this new Law is in many respects similar to the BSHG but significantly differs in others. Most importantly, it stipulates that asylum seekers should be given benefits in kind (e.g. clothing) rather than cash. However, some local authorities continue to pay out in cash.

In order to achieve the aims of *Sozialhilfe* the BSHG commits welfare offices to advise claimants of their rights. However, it can be assumed that many potentially eligible recipients do not make a claim due to a number of factors (lack of information, fear of social stigma, inability or unwillingness to deal with social bureaucracy etc).

In principle, there is no local flexibility as to coverage or variation among groups of claimants. However, individual circumstances are crucial in determining the level and type of support. Furthermore, the BSHG distinguishes between so-called 'must', 'should' and 'can' benefits and regulations. The first type ('must') is required by law without exception (for example, benefit rates cannot be reduced by local offices). The second type ('should') can only be rejected or restricted if there are serious reasons which can be scrutinised by courts. It is the 'can' type which allows local welfare offices a wide scope of discretion in the implementation of *Sozialhilfe*. However, administrative guidelines (*Sozialhilferichtlinien*), which are issued at Land and municipality levels, specify limits to the extent of discretion. These guidelines aim to harmonize the implementation of *Sozialhilfe* in a particular *Land*. Although not legally binding, they have an important impact on the actual interpretation of the BSHG within individual *Länder* and are crucial for the implementation of *Sozialhilfe* by individual welfare officers. They are also a major reason for variations between regions, which can be considerable.

For example, local welfare offices in one region might offer more, and a wider variety of, job and training offers to unemployed *Sozialhilfe* recipients than other regions. Some local authorities go further than others when it comes to approaching relatives who are obliged to provide maintenance for the *Sozialhilfe* applicant. There are also many variations regarding one-off payments for single items such as furniture, clothing, flat renovations etc. Most of these payments are required by law, and the German Association (an umbrella organisation of local and regional welfare authorities) issues recommendations about the level of payments. However, in the last instance it is up to local welfare offices to fix the value, the nature and the frequency of grants. For example, some welfare offices allow recipients grants for a winter coat more frequently and at higher levels than others. Furniture is provided by some local authorities in kind, relying on either new or second-hand material, while others pay out grants. Some local authorities allow for TV sets, others exclude them. Christmas Aid for recipients of *Sozialhilfe* is higher in some regions than in others. Also, some regions (and some individual officers) take their duty to inform applicants more seriously than others (see *Sozialhilferechtlinien*, 1995). Whether this is a deliberate strategy or due to lack of resources, insufficient knowledge about *Sozialhilfe* rights is another way of keeping expenditure down. It should be added however, that the *Sozialhilfe* 'culture' (eg the density of self-help groups, welfare associations etc.) is more developed in some regions than in others, thus helping to increase recipient's awareness about entitlements. As noted below, when compared with the UK, the welfare rights lobby is just beginning to develop.

Sozialhilfe and the local economy

Local circumstances are crucially important for *Sozialhilfe*. A high demand for rented accommodation increases rents and consequently *Sozialhilfe* payments. Unemployment has become a major cause for many applications for benefit. Some regions are more affected than others by labour market and economic restructuring. This means that the number of people without unemployment insurance coverage is likely to be higher and the pressure on *Sozialhilfe* expenditure greater in some regions than in others. One classic response by local authorities has been to provide job contracts mostly in the public sector (as, for example, secretaries, nurse helpers or porters) which last for one year, enabling *Sozialhilfe* recipients to accumulate sufficient credits in order to become eligible for insurance benefit once they are made redundant again. Another response has been the provision of, or subsidy to, a variety of job creation, training and employment schemes as well as wage subsidies for employers who take on *Sozialhilfe* recipients. These, often innovative, programmes have been adopted by many local authorities to different degrees. Variations can be explained by the lack of jobs, the fear of creating adverse competition with private companies, different financial capacities and the political will to make efforts to reintegrate long-term unemployed people. The disciplinary option to restrict benefit payments if suitable job offers are declined is not extensively applied at present, although the federal government would like to change this.

According to respondents, only a few local authorities evaluate these integrative schemes relatively extensively and frequently. For example, a recent study investigated the efficiency and effectiveness of the so called 'aid to work' programme for unemployed *Sozialhilfe* recipients in Bremen (Jakobs, 1995). Evaluations are sporadic, however, and at times only conducted internally (i.e. by providing training or work experience programmes themselves with or without financial support from the local authority).

Unlike traditional labour market schemes for which the Federal Labour Office and local employment offices are responsible, there is no nationwide evaluation of these local programmes. Another crucial difference is that federal programmes are predominantly for recipients of unemployment insurance benefits rather than *Sozialhilfe*. Programmes provided (or commissioned) by the Federal Labour Office are mainly for recipients of unemployment benefit or unemployment assistance (that is, former contributors to, or current claimants of insurance related benefits. Local social assistance offices end up with those who are (predominantly) without insurance based benefit.

Sensitivity to circumstances

Different family circumstances (number and age of children) are crucial since they determine the level of *Sozialhilfe* for the household. Some applicants receive supplements (eg pregnant women, people of retirement age, lone parents) and people in remunerative work are granted a disregard on their earnings (see BSHG, 1994).

The degree of central guidance in local flexibility and the way it is expressed and communicated has been described above (page 24). Amendments to the BSHG and their interpretations are communicated via so-called administrative orders (*Verwaltungsanweisungen*) to local welfare officers who have to study and acknowledge them. There is also an extensive system of further training which aims to increase and keep up-to-date the expertise of local officers in order to guarantee a uniform application of the BSHG.

There is no periodical reassessment of claims for *Sozialhilfe*. However, recipients are required by law to indicate any personal or material changes in their circumstances so that benefits can be adjusted accordingly. Also, when legislation changes, forms have to be checked and altered as well as benefit levels when they are uprated (usually every 6 to 12 months). Checks on individual claims may be made dependent on the judgement of local officers who might ask claimants to come for an interview. There is even the option of checking up on claimants by visiting them in their homes. This is hardly ever done in practice.

Geographical equity

There are no geographical differences in law as far as *Sozialhilfe* is concerned. However, differences in custom and practice exist especially in the area of one-off payments. These are based on different interpretations of the BSHG between *Länder* and also between individual welfare officers. Except for Bavaria, standard benefit levels are almost identical in the old *Länder*. In the new *Länder* they are lower and more differentiated due to political decisions made at the time of German unification and the indexation of benefit rates since then. However, it should be noted that the latter can be larger between big cities and rural areas within a single Land than between two *Länder*. This is the reason why a few cities, eg Munich, have their own benefit levels, which are above those stipulated for the *Land*. Other differences apply to the overall *Sozialhilfe* payment per head which includes costs for accommodation and one-off payments. Other factors are variations in the availability of jobs, benefits and services in the region provided by voluntary welfare organisations, the degree of take-up, customs of paying out one-off payments but also differences in what could be called local *Sozialhilfe* mentalities; ie. the readiness to seek help from local welfare offices which varies between the North and the South, between young and old and between large cities and small communities with a higher degree of social control. Although the Basic Law requires a uniformity of 'life chances' throughout the country, differences in standard benefit rates are not a source of controversy (presumably since they have become very small). By contrast, differences in one-off payments (which, unlike the British Social Fund are not ring-fenced) are a matter of debate, but only among Social Assistance experts and officials. Also, the German Association makes recommendations about individual payments. Finally, the government is currently trying to legislate for more uniform rates of one-off payments throughout the country in order to exert greater influence/control over aggregate levels of expenditure.

Stigma/peer pressure

The cause of the stigma associated with *Sozialhilfe* does not lie with local administration or discretionary decisions. Far more important, according to respondents, is the application of the means-test, including the recourse to relatives obliged to pay maintenance (about which there is little firm evidence). It is the needs-orientation of *Sozialhilfe* which is contrary to the tradition of German social security, dominated by social insurance and based on principles of reciprocity and restitution which causes the greatest offence. Stigmatisation, it could be argued, applies to those who previously have not contributed to their support.

According to previous studies, the take-up rate of *Sozialhilfe* by eligible claimants was about 50 per cent in the early 1980s (Hartmann, 1985). There has been no systematic and comprehensive research into take-up since then. According to estimates, however, the rate has increased in line with an increase in the overall number of *Sozialhilfe* recipients. Stigmatisation can be assumed to be a major factor for non take-up but whether this is an objective of policy would be hard to prove. Recent qualitative studies of *Sozialhilfe* recipients suggest that the scheme is still associated with feelings of shame, stigmatisation and even discrimination (Leibfried and Leisering, 1995). However, there are differences between recipients. Younger people and those with better qualifications are more likely to apply for *Sozialhilfe* and more likely (than older people) to consider it as something 'normal'. There is geographical variation in attitudes towards claiming Sozialhilfe.

Whether *Sozialhilfe* is regarded as a fair and non-discriminating benefit is hard to judge and answers vary according to the person being asked (recipients, welfare officers, general public). In a recent survey, many recipients criticised the scheme but considered treatment by individual officers as being fair. Officials who exercise discretion in accordance with the law and administrative guidelines regard their actions as fair. It is possible to divide the public into those who consider *Sozialhilfe* to be too low and discriminating and those who regard it as too generous and lenient, inviting fraudulent claims.

There is little knowledge, at a national level, of recipients' perceptions of *Sozialhilfe* as a whole and there is a lack of statistical information about other aspects such as the duration of *Sozialhilfe* spells at the federal level. This has frequently been criticised by researchers and experts, who have demanded periodical poverty reports similar to existing family and health reports published by the government. More information about recipients is available on the local level but, once again, some local authorities are more active than others. Bremen, for example, has conducted and commissioned research into claimant satisfaction.

As far as a welfare rights lobby is concerned, the situation in Germany is different from that in the UK. There is certainly not the same type of welfare rights tradition and there is no equivalent to the CPAG - but then again, poverty is a subject which has entered the public domain only recently. The first local poverty reports were written in the 1980s. However, there are a number of self-help initiatives among *Sozialhilfe* recipients in local areas as well as an umbrella organisation at the federal level. They provide advice and most of them receive some sort of financial support from local authorities or welfare offices directly. Then there are the six big voluntary welfare organisations, of which the church-related ones (*Caritas* and *Diakonisches Werk*) and the umbrella association of small independent organisations (*Deutscher Paritätischer Wohlfahrtsverband*) are the most active - also in terms of trying to influence government opinion. The two big churches themselves (especially the Protestant church) also see themselves as acting politically on behalf of marginalised social groups. Some trades unions have recently 'discovered' that *Sozialhilfe* policy is of importance and the Greens are the political party which is most active in the 'poverty arena'. Indeed it can be argued that social welfare offices on local and Land level see themselves as some sort of 'lobby' for *Sozialhilfe* recipients - although only up to a point since they, as a public administration, are supposed to be apolitical. However, respondents pointed out that all these organisations are much less effective in support of *Sozialhilfe* recipients compared with the lobby acting on behalf of disabled people.

Appeals and redress

Claimants have the right of appeal. In the first instance they have the right to speak to the line manager of the welfare officer who has rejected a claim. A second step would be to make a written appeal which might be formulated with the help of an advice centre. This appeal is part of an administrative procedure which is processed by a special appeal section within the welfare office. In the case of a rejection, the next option would be to take the issue to the appropriate administrative court, for which legal aid is normally granted.

There are no country-wide statistics about numbers, reasons or outcomes of appeals. However, some welfare offices have internal statistics since particular sections deal with appeal cases. According to respondents, there are indications that one-off payments figure prominently as a main reason for appeals and geographical differences in the number of appeals can be assumed.

Simplicity

Discretionary decisions and local differences in granting one-off payments perhaps make the system less easy to understand for recipients and therefore less transparent. However, this situation is improving as are standard benefit rates within a single Land are established and many one-off payments which have been standardised, wherever feasible, not least in order to reduce costs. Whether localisation makes the system more cost-effective overall is hard to judge because of the impossibility of calculating administrative costs per case.

Control of fraud

Abuse of *Sozialhilfe* is a topic of discussion in Germany. Internal checks of files suggest a small minority of about 3 to 10 per cent of 'irregular' or 'unclear' cases, which might not be caused by fraudulent intent but by misinformation or uncertainty about claimants' entitlements both on the side of recipients and individual officers alike (see Von Fintel and Wagner, 1989). Other estimates suggest a rate of up to 25 per cent fraudulent claims. These estimates have to be taken cautiously however since they are not scientifically proven and often associated with interests which seek to play down or play up the extent of fraud.

Exact figures based on comprehensive studies do not exist.

One of the main types of fraudulent claim is probably the non-declaration of some form of additional income. According to officials, however, the amount of money involved is often relatively small. Fraud is monitored by individual officers who can invite claimants for interviews to discuss their cases. The computerisation of files also allows welfare offices to double-check claims with neighbouring welfare offices in order to prevent multiple claims. Furthermore, since 1993 the BSHG has allowed welfare offices to access personal data held by other public agencies so that, for example, the receipt of other types of social security transfers or the possession of a car can be checked easily.

Anti-fraud campaigns organised by welfare offices are very rare but have happened in some *Länder* in the past. More common are campaigns by local employment offices who organise spot checks on building sites and restaurants in particular. The aim is to detect illegal employment: *Sozialhilfe* recipients not declaring their earnings are among those who are found out.

Within the administration, and among officials, fraud is not regarded as a major problem. Within political debate, however, suspected fraud is an issue and the government is currently in the process of implementing a BSHG reform which also involves new sanctions for fraudulent behaviour. Most importantly, all welfare offices will be expected to reduce standard benefit rates (*Regelsätze*) by 'at least' 25 per cent if claimants have refused suitable offers of employment or programmes for the reintegration in the labour market. At present, the imposition of this sanction is at the discretion of local offices.

Pressure points and policy options

The German government has proposed a number of changes to the BSHG which are currently being debated (*Deutscher Bundestag*, 1995). Some of the issues need further specification and, more importantly, have to be accepted by the *Bundesrat* before they can become law (probably in July 1996). Yet the direction of change is clear. Local authorities will be expected to make more effort regarding unemployed claimants. More jobs and placement offers are to be combined with a more rigorous use of disciplinary actions against those claimants who refuse offers. The legislation is also likely to transfer competency for determining standard benefit rates from *Länder* to the Federal government. With a view to establishing firmer control over expenditure a national standardisation of one-off payments is proposed as well.

Finally, and perhaps most controversially, the government would like local authorities to apply the 'wage rule' more forcefully. According to this rule, benefit levels in a particular *Land* have to be set so that the total income of a family with three children receiving *Sozialhilfe* is below the average net income (including benefits) of an equivalent family with one earner on low wages. According to interview sources, whenever this principle was in conflict (normally it is not) with the principle according to which *Sozialhilfe* aims at covering needs based on the cost of living, local authorities tended to give greater weight to the latter. It appears the government would like to change this so that local authorities would have to decide in favour of the wage rule instead.

Advantages

Positive aspects of *Sozialhilfe* mentioned by officials and experts are the scheme's decentralised organisation, the principle of 'individualisation' (including the scope of discretionary decision making), the legal codification of entitlements, the level of assistance granted to families and the speed with which claims are administered and payments made. Furthermore, recent studies show that a major aim of the scheme, to enable recipients to overcome the dependence on *Sozialhilfe*, is actually achieved by the large majority of claimants (Ludwig et al, 1995).

Disadvantages

Negative aspects mentioned were the lack of information on some aspects of *Sozialhilfe*. For example, the duration of individual *Sozialhilfe* spells is only beginning to be monitored, while local authorities have to make individual efforts in order to find out how other *Länder* deal with the same issues (eg the payment of particular one-off grants). The degree of means-testing and especially the wide definition of mutual responsibility for maintenance between relatives has also been criticised. In addition, within many local authorities *Sozialhilfe* appears to maintain its residual character with local authority officers apparently reluctant to transfer to *Sozialhilfe* duties because staff and buildings are regarded as being of inferior quality.

The main problem is the growth in *Sozialhilfe* dependency. The Bremen studies (Jakobs, 1995) indicate that whereas the total number of recipients has increased, a majority are claimants for only a short period. Contrary to its intention, *Sozialhilfe* has become an income transfer which is not only crucially important for a growing minority of the population, it increasingly also covers so-called 'standard risks' of life (eg unemployment, maternity) which are supposed to be the responsibility of other forms of public help (social insurance, family policy). The inadequacy of the latter policies has meant that problems and financial consequences have gradually but steadily been transferred from the federal to the local level. The difficulty local authorities face in funding *Sozialhilfe* has become a major pressure point in the system.

4 The Netherlands

The Netherlands is a medium sized country with a population of approximately 15.3 million. Although it has a fertility rate which is below replacement rate, it is above the European average at 1.57 in 1993. It has a relatively young population profile and approximately 10 per cent of all families with dependent children are headed by a lone parent. It has a moderately successful economy and is regarded as providing one of the most comprehensive and generous social protection systems in the EU. However, historically high levels of labour productivity have sustained a relatively high proportion of social security dependants: for every four Dutch employees there are three full-time benefit recipients. There is a relatively low level of female economic participation and rising levels of unemployment (and, in particular, long term unemployment).

The Netherlands is a decentralised unitary state. There is a three tier hierarchical structure consisting of state, province and municipality. Provinces are represented at the national level in the first chamber of parliament, to which they elect members.

Table 4.1 Numbers of authorities by tier of government (1994)

Tier	No. of authorities	Population
Level 1	1	15.23 million
Level 2 - provinces	12	225,000 - 3.3 million
Level 3 - municipalities*	646	933 - 590,000

Amsterdam and Rotterdam are sub-divided into 17+11 sub-municipalities respectively.

Source: Hollis et al. 1994. p.93.

Within each province, governance is the responsibility of an assembly, an executive and a Queen's Commissioner. At each tier of government there is considerable variation in the size of population.

Dutch local authorities (municipalities) have dual functions: they either act as agents for the national government or else have *de facto* autonomy. In practice they are more like agents than independent actors. This is largely because more than 40 per cent of local authority income is provided in the form of government grants from the centre. Increasingly this has been in the form of service specific payments rather than a general block grant.

The municipalities are responsible for the following services: education and welfare; sport and recreation; social policy: unemployment and social benefits, social work; local health services; public works and housing; local police and civil defence. The largest proportion of expenditure at this level (31.7 per cent) is committed to social services and welfare, followed by housing (17.8 per cent) and then education (10.7 per cent).

When a municipality cannot balance its budget it can apply for what is known as Article 12 status (ie *de facto* bankruptcy) (Financial Distribution Act 1984). However central control over the use of the budget has increased so applications for this status have declined: down from 159 in 1969 to 25 in 1987.

Since the early 1980s the Netherlands has sought to re-think the scope and responsibilities of government (at all levels). Hollis *et al* argue that in response to a succession of budget crises, a strategy involving decentralisation, deregulation, privatisation and down-sizing has been pursued, (Hollis *et al* 1994 p. 104). A process of rationalization is also being implemented. As part of the ongoing debate about the structure of sub-national government, the Union of Dutch Municipalities (*Vereniging van Nederlandse Gemeeken*: an association representing all local authorities) has proposed the reduction in number of municipalities from 646 to 70, in order to improve the efficiency of service delivery.

Throughout the 1980s, and with the exception of Sweden, the Netherlands (among OECD nations) committed the highest proportion of its GDP to social protection. In 1991, expenditure on social security (excluding health costs) was estimated at 22.3 per cent of GDP, compared with an EU average of 16.9 per cent. The Netherlands is a country committed to the pursuit of equality and has achieved a degree of success in this objective. However, between 1980 and 1990 the number of households living on the 'social minimum' grew from 300,000 to 900,000.

Aims and structure of social assistance

The Dutch Social Assistance scheme aims to provide financial assistance to all legal residents who cannot adequately provide for the necessary costs of living of his/her household (Kemperman, 1994). More specifically, the objective of ABW (General Assistance) is to provide a guaranteed income, while at the same time preventing long-term dependency and providing some integration.

Minimum levels of income are guaranteed by the state for all Dutch citizens under the National Assistance Act (ABW), the Act on Income Provisions for Older and Partially Disabled Workers (IOAW), the Act on Income Provisions for Older and Partially Disabled Formerly Self-Employed (IOAZ) and the Supplementary Benefits Act (TW). Social Assistance schemes are supervised by the Minister for Social Affairs and Employment, implemented by the municipalities and managed by the Union of Dutch Municipalities (VNG). Municipalities also take additional measures to prevent social isolation of the lowest income families. These include local schemes to provide advice and information, to help people settle their debt problems and to find work, as well as local schemes to provide direct cash assistance (Kemperman, 1994).

The social minimum income is central to Dutch social security and was introduced in 1974. It is based on the legally prescribed net minimum wage for full-time workers for two adults living together, with or without children (Table 4.2). Special rates apply to couples where one partner is under 21, single people under 23 and school leavers aged 21 to 27 years.

Table 4.2   Social minimum income as a percentage of the minimum wage

Family Type	% of Minimum Wage
(Un) married couples (same or different genders)	100
Single parent families	90
Single people living alone	70
Single people sharing accommodation	60

[Adapted from Kemperman, 1994]

Every Dutch citizen is guaranteed an income from national schemes to at least the level of the social minimum. This is achieved mainly through two contributory, non-means-tested insurance schemes - National or 'Peoples'

Insurance paid at a flat rate in cases of old age or death and earnings-related Employees or 'Workers' Insurance which covers sickness, unemployment and disability. In 1990, 85 per cent of benefit recipients had payments from social insurance schemes (Kemperman, 1994).

In relation to these insurance-based schemes, means-tested Social Assistance acts as a safety-net, providing incomes for people living on less than the social minimum. Its main components are General Unemployment Assistance (RWW) and General Assistance (ABW). These provide monthly payments to cover normal living costs: this excludes 'special' costs such as those related to medical and social services; sickness and disability; training, work experience and finding employment. In addition, and in common with many Dutch benefits, there is a holiday allowance equivalent to about 8 per cent of the main monthly amount (Table 4.3). Other assistance benefits are provided for specific groups of people. IOAW provides assistance for older or incapacitated unemployed people and IOAZ for the unemployed aged 55 to 65 who were formerly self-employed. Supplementary Benefit (TW) can also be regarded as a form of Social Assistance since, although it is paid only under employee insurance schemes and is administered by social insurance councils, its role is to supplement existing payments up to the social minimum.

Although the main aim of Social Assistance is to guarantee that all citizens receive at least the social minimum income, the National Assistance Act is formulated with the additional aim of supporting the integration of recipients into the labour market through exemption rules for earned income and through assistance to help with expenses incurred on routes into work. Also included in the Act is Special Assistance (BB) to provide cash help for exceptional needs. This benefit is not restricted to Social Assistance recipients but can be applied for by anyone with a low net balance between income (irrespective of source) and certain fixed expenses.

Centre-local relationships

National legislation governs Social Assistance but the schemes are implemented by municipalities. Since the National Assistance Act of 1963, local authorities have been specifically required to provide assistance to any Dutch national without the means to support him or herself. The schemes are financed through taxation and rates of benefit are fixed nationally in relation to the minimum wage.

There is no local variation in decisions about who is eligible for assistance or in the basic rates payable. Some small differences may occur in the total level of payments awarded depending on the information made available to local social services and the extent to which they apply rules about availability for work. The availability of work in different regions may influence the latter. Although differences are marginal, local policies on housing and shelter for example may determine to which city homeless people go to claim benefits.

In response to growing numbers of recipients and increased long-term dependency on Social Assistance during the 1980s, a revised National Assistance Act was put before Parliament, first in 1992 and again in 1994. Changes in legislation were designed to reduce expenditure by tighter targeting of benefits and reducing fraud, modernise the law, encourage people to earn their own living and to extend the responsibilities of local authorities. The new Act, implemented in January 1996, rationalises differences between general Social Assistance for the unemployed and for other groups in a single new benefit, ABW.

Table 4.3   Benefit rates for Social Assistance (per month), January 1993, in Dutch Guilders and £ sterling equivalents, adjusted by purchasing power parities

	Basic	+Holiday Allowances	Total in £ppps
Couple (married or cohabiting)			
both over 21	1760.31	92.26	537
one or both under 21, maximum per person	880.16	48.14	269
Lone parents			
over 21	1584.28	86.63	484
under 21 living independently	1549.46	84.76	473
under 21 living with parents	1151.20	62.95	351
Single person (not sharing)			
23 or over	1232.22	69.52	377
22	1028.79	56.33	314
21	899.03	49.19	274
under 21 or school leaver	860.81	47.09	263
under 21 and living at home	462.55	25.30	141

It gives more autonomy to municipalities, enabling them to attach supplementary conditions to benefit payments with a view to providing incentives to recipients to find paid employment: this has been necessary to bring financial arrangements into line with decentralised responsibilities for the delivery of benefits. Under the new system local authorities are provided with the instruments to adjust part of Social Assistance payments to their own local standards. The basic amount of benefit payable to a single person is reduced to 50 per cent of the minimum wage and the basic amount for a lone parent is reduced from 90 to 70 per cent. Municipal authorities have a legal **responsibility** to supplement the basic amount by up to 20 per cent but must use their discretion in deciding the exact amount to be awarded. Where lone parents and single adults can prove that they do not share living costs with another adult they receive the maximum addition of 20 per cent so that their total amount of assistance is equal to 90 and 70 per cent of the minimum wage respectively, as before.

These moves to give municipalities more discretion reflects a trend towards decentralisation which began in the late 1980s following an earlier period of centralisation. The introduction of the social minimum in 1974 and the national standardisation of means tests for general and special assistance were a central government response to stem increasing variation in the application of discretion at municipal level during the 1960s. National guidelines were issued from the centre in attempts to equalise citizens' minimum income rights and to form a base for developing a national income policy (van Oorschot and Smolenaars, 1993). In this context, the current trend is not without apparent contradictions.

The devolution of more discretionary powers to municipalities has so far been accompanied by other government moves which act to constrain the application of discretion. During the 1980s municipalities expanded the development of local assistance policies in response to social problems stemming from the financial difficulties increasingly experienced by a growing number of households living at minimum income level. These included the use of municipal funds to help people with, for example, educational expenses, debts or special needs, as well as policies to exempt certain people from local taxation. These schemes are thought to play an important role in offering security to the lowest income households but there is considerable variation in the presence and content of local policies. Depending on the local political climate and on population size and composition, different municipalities have set their own objectives and target groups for assistance (van Oorschot and Smolenaars, 1993). There is no national obligation of provision but orders from central government now oblige municipalities to apply the 'principle of individualisation' so that a benefit can only be paid after considering all the circumstances of each individual applicant. This limits discretion by precluding provision of municipal assistance to whole categories of people and at least partly contributes to the high administration costs and low take-up rates of municipal schemes (van Oorschot, 1995).

There are a range of local municipal taxes including an estate tax (based mainly on the size of a dwelling); a sewerage tax; garbage tax and a dog tax. Before 1991, estate tax was collected by the national tax office but the municipalities administered and collected other taxes. They were able to apply generous exemption policies on sewerage, garbage and dog taxes.

With the introduction of the New Collecting Act (1991), municipalities also administer and collect estate tax. However, the Act lays down strict rules for tax exemption for all local taxes, such that the number of eligible households has declined sharply. The income assistance policies of local authorities are thus more limited than previously (van Oorschot and Smolenaars, 1993).

The case of Special Assistance (BB), to meet exceptional needs, provides a further example of the apparently ambiguous attitude of central government towards local authorities. Municipalities are obliged to offer the possibility of Special Assistance but within the national structure of regulations and nationally determined scale rates, local social workers employed by municipalities have a considerable degree of discretion in making payments. Before 1991, 90 per cent of the cost of the scheme was met by central government but municipalities were free to decide exactly which expenses were 'special' and how much should be paid. The decentralisation of the scheme in 1991 aimed to target Special Assistance more effectively on people in real need by giving more discretion to local authorities. Central regulations and guidelines were abolished but the 90 per cent central funding mechanism was also removed. Municipalities must now operate the scheme within the limits of a fixed annual lump sum which places restrictions on the kinds and amounts of payments made.

The decentralisation of Social Assistance appears to be devolving more financial and discretionary responsibility onto municipalities while at the same time placing increased constraints on the budgets or guidelines within which they must operate. The Netherlands municipalities play a major role in ensuring the well-being of their citizens and, particularly in the larger cities, have their own contacts with members of Parliament. Their influence on central government policy-making is exercised by providing advice or lobbying, either as individual authorities or collectively through VNG (the Union of Dutch Municipalities) and DIVOSA (the Union of Directors of Municipal Social Services).

The VNG is the main body for liaising between municipalities and central government and has regular contact with the Minister for Social Affairs. The new Social Assistance legislation arose after a long period of consultation and co-operation between central government and the VNG representing local authority interests. In 1994, central government established a new body (LVO) to oversee the quality of service and delivery of benefits during the first three years of the new scheme.

Finance and control

The funds for Social Assistance are raised through taxation. Before 1996, 90 per cent of costs of ABW (General Social Assistance), RWW (Unemployment Benefit), IOAW (Benefit for Older and Partially Disabled Workers) and IOAZ (Benefit for Older and Partially Disabled Workers: Formerly Self-Employed) were paid by central government and 10 per cent by local authorities. There were no limits on budgets in this open-ended financing structure. In addition, central government funds 100 per cent of expenditure on TW and Special Assistance but the latter is paid to municipalities as a fixed annual block amount added to the general fund (*Gemeentefonds*) of each municipality.

From 1996, the discretionary additions to the basic amount of assistance (ABW) also have to be paid from the *Gemeentefonds* and for this purpose an additional fixed sum is allocated to each municipality from the centre. Other sources of local authority funding are local taxation and ear-marked central government payments which are contingent upon municipalities increasing labour market participation. After a three-year period of adjustment, local authorities must take full responsibility for meeting discretionary additions to Social Assistance.

Nationally the administration costs of general Social Assistance constituted 8.2 per cent of the total awarded in 1990 (CBS, 1993). In contrast a study of local provision in the city of Nijmegen shows average administration costs of a quarter of the amount awarded (van Oorschot and Smolenaars, 1993).

Local authority expenditure is monitored and audited first by municipality accountants, secondly by accountants in the Department of Social Affairs and finally by the '*Algemene Rekenkamer*' (Department of Accounts) on behalf of Parliament. Overspending is only possible where Social Assistance payments have been made to ineligible claimants, where Special Assistance payments amount to more than allowed by the fixed block grants or, since 1996, where additional discretionary payments exceed expected levels. After a three year adjustment period municipalities will have to meet all surplus costs from their own funds.

Social Assistance and the local economy

Various schemes at a local level attempt to (re)integrate recipients of Social Assistance into the labour market. The Youth Employment Guarantee Act (1992) requires municipalities to find or create jobs to provide work experience for all unemployed 16 to 21 year olds and for school-leavers aged 23 and over.

In return for 32 hours work a week, young people receive the Youth Minimum Wage. The low demand for labour has been blamed for the lack of success of this scheme. Many municipalities find it impossible to create enough places while in other areas places remain unfilled because unemployed young people in the locality are unsuited to the work available. As a result, the schemes often succeed in placing only the most 'employable' young people. Substantial numbers are paid the minimum wage without actually participating in the Youth Job Guarantee Scheme, thus weakening any potential incentive effects (Evidence collected by Eardley et al, 1996). Municipalities have recently received warnings from central government, demanding that they make greater efforts to ensure that the scheme operates as intended.

The municipal social services and Regional Manpower Board* also have an obligation to work towards the reintegration of people who have been unemployed for 3 years or more. They must organise 'reorientation' interviews with a view to establishing plans for helping people re-enter the labour market. Municipalities have been given resources to develop this scheme to enhance the job-prospects of clients but its potential is still limited by low local levels of demand for labour.

---

* The Regional Manpower Board has regional employment offices where unemployed assistance recipients must be registered. These offices are separate from the municipalities.

Recipients of RWW and ABW, except for lone parents with a child younger than five years old, must be 'seeking work' and are obliged to accept any suitable employment offered. Work is allowed while receiving Social Assistance and, until 1994, national rules ensured that 25 per cent of earned income was disregarded in means-testing up to a limit of 15 per cent of benefit payable. An extra 15 per cent was disregarded for lone parents. Training and retraining schemes could also be undertaken as long as they were linked to regular employment. Since July 1994, municipalities in consultation with the Regional Manpower Boards have been given increased powers to stimulate labour market participation. Money has been made available, for example, to give premiums to recipients of Social Assistance who participate in education or work. Local governments are now responsible for formulating their own policies on earnings disregards.

Coverage and sensitivity to circumstances

Dutch citizens and legal residents can claim Social Assistance as a right from the age of 18 (unemployed) or 21 (others) up to the age of 65, as long as they are otherwise unable to meet their basic subsistence needs. Although there are specific provisions for certain unemployed and disabled people (IOAW, IOAZ) there are none for lone parents, who receive benefits under ABW, the new general scheme guaranteeing minimum incomes. Before 1996, RWW for the unemployed was the dominant scheme. The number of beneficiaries was nearly twice as high as that for ABW. In 1993, 314.7 thousand families were receiving RWW compared with 168.5 thousand receiving ABW.

Eligibility is based on households and the 'benefit unit' includes any spouse or partner as well as children under 21 years old. Payments are generally made to the applicant but may be shared between partners if requested. Assistance is both means-tested and asset-tested. Net income, children's income and investment income within limits and other social security benefits are all taken into account. Training allowances, gifts and charity payments may be exempted depending on the situation and any alimony or child maintenance payments are disregarded. Capital, savings and property are dealt with according to a system of thresholds and exemptions.

Eligibility for Social Assistance is reviewed, on average, every 8 months (evidence collected by Eardley et al, 1996). Any changes in income, living conditions, family conditions, education, assets and availability for the labour market which occur in the meantime must be reported without delay to the relevant office. Recipients who are required to be seeking work should be registered with the Regional Manpower Board and have to report on a monthly basis.

Although most respondents (see acknowledgements) in this study said that Social Assistance benefits do in general go to those for whom they are intended, one respondent pointed out that the main recipients were supposed to be people requiring assistance for short periods of time. 'Nowadays for most of our clients it is an everlasting basic income, until the age of 65 is reached'. Another recognised the difficulty of proving that a client purporting to live alone is actually cohabiting and accepted that some such claimants may be receiving more benefits than those to which they are entitled. There seems to be little need for local targeting activities. Since it represents a last resort, people are expected to 'come and get it' as otherwise they would have to live below subsistence level.

There is little evidence of differential treatment afforded to different groups of claimants although social services are thought by one respondent in this study to be less strict in their assessments for lone parents. They may also vary in the ways in which they check on whether claimants are actively seeking work. From 1996 municipalities must provide plans detailing their activities to help more people to find work. Their increasing role in encouraging labour market participation may lead to more local flexibility in dealing with the unemployed.

There is some resistance on the part of municipalities to considering claimants as 'groups' rather than individuals. Nevertheless, some claimants such as the homeless or drug addicts do get special attention. Under the new regulations the requirement for local implementation of the 'principle of individualisation' will be relaxed but the extent and impact of this change is not yet clear.

People are only left without assistance in extreme cases, for example when a homeless person has no formal registration address or makes no claim or when someone repeatedly refuses to accept paid work with no 'reasonable' explanation. One respondent pointed to the distinction between being left without benefit because of the law and because of a personal preference for a particular lifestyle. Non-nationals with no legal entitlement to benefit may receive assistance in emergencies.

Geographical equity

The main elements of Social Assistance in the Netherlands are governed by national regulations and nationally set scale rates, ensuring equality of treatment across local municipalities. Recent changes, however, are devolving more discretionary responsibility to municipal level, increasing the potential for geographical variation in the future.

Stigma/Peer Pressure

Stigmatisation related to means-testing is not generally regarded as an important issue in the Netherlands and there is little public debate on the subject. It is recognised that, for people who need it, Social Assistance is a right to which they are entitled. The prevailing culture views dependency on benefits as a result of societal processes rather than personal failure or deviance. There is, however, some resistance, particularly from the women's movement, to the means-testing of partners since this, it is argued, leads to disincentives for partners to look for work. These disincentives act, along with other factors, to influence the participation in the labour market of women who live with partners in receipt of means-tested benefits (evidence collected by Eardley et al, 1996).

The government does not publish estimates of non-take-up and no national measures are taken to encourage take-up of benefits. Research has shown that people generally are aware of their entitlement to general Social Assistance but that there only low levels of awareness about special assistance and local schemes (such as exemptions from property tax, garbage tax or dog tax). Non-take-up rates of between 25 and 75 per cent have been found for these supplements to general assistance and local take-up campaigns have been largely ineffective. This is thought to be due to the difficulties of providing adequate information about benefits which cover such a wide range of circumstances and individual needs. The evidence suggests, however, that feelings of shame or humiliation play only a minor role in explaining non-take-up of housing benefit, special assistance and assistance from local schemes (van Oorschot and Smolenaars, 1993; van Oorschot, 1995).

Social Assistance is generally seen by study respondents as a fair system except where a partner's income is assumed to be available to a potential claimant for the purpose of means-testing. It is thought that some claimants may perceive unfairness in certain aspects, such as the application of earnings disregards, the obligations on lone parents to look for work and the different possibilities for following educational or training courses. There are, however, no visible municipal differences as yet leading to claimant complaints of unfairness.

Claimants' views are made known informally through their contacts with administrators and, formally, through the client councils established by some larger municipalities. These can sometimes provide effective means of ensuring that claimants' views are taken seriously but there is wide variation between municipalities. There are no official national surveys but some local social surveys have asked claimants about their opinions on and experiences with social services. In Amsterdam for example a 'clients' satisfaction survey' is carried out annually.

Appeals and redress

Applicants who are not satisfied can challenge decisions made about Social Assistance claims under the General Law on Administrative Appeal. The law covers the exercise of administrative discretion as well as points of legal interpretation. Claimants must write to the municipal social welfare office within one month of the original decision, outlining the grounds for complaint. In most cases where there is any *prima facie* possibility of an incorrect decision, claimants have a right to an informal hearing at municipal level. In some authorities this internal review may be carried out by a special committee. If the claimant is still not satisfied by the outcome, an appeal can be made to the regional court which, since a judicial re-organisation in 1994, has a special chamber for hearing administrative appeals.

There are no centrally collected statistics about appeals against Social Assistance but it is expected that under the new legislation this omission is likely to change.

There is no coherent, influential poverty lobby in the Netherlands. *De Arme Kant van Nederland* (The Poor Side of the Netherlands) is an organisation which holds symposia, demonstrations and other actions to raise public awareness but its activities are only sporadic and the influence of the group is limited. Some local organisations exist to address the problems of particular interest groups such as women or disabled workers. Although some of these are co-ordinated by central committees, they do not cooperate strongly together on the whole and have no major influence on national policy.

Simplicity

The localisation of Social Assistance is not regarded as having promoted simplicity, made schemes easier to understand or easier to administer. The emphasis on local decisions about individual circumstances might, however, make decisions easier to explain to claimants.

The new legislation requires every municipality to develop its own scheme but it is thought by respondents that adjustments will be made to fit in with other authorities and this is likely to lead to more complexity. The difficulties faced by claimants include, for example, assessing the impacts which part-time earnings are likely to have on benefit status, a problem which is unlikely to be resolved under the new system. In the case of Special Assistance many municipalities have continued to apply the national rules and guidelines which were in force before de-centralisation. Alternatively, they have developed their own, equally complex, guidelines.

Control of fraud

An informal distinction is made between three types of Social Assistance fraud in the Netherlands. 'White' fraud refers to the receipt of assistance while having unreported earnings from official work and has recently been reduced to negligible levels since the linking of social services computer files with those of tax and national insurance offices. A national identity card must be shown when an initial claim for benefit is made.

'Black' fraud occurs when benefit recipients have unreported earnings from work in the 'black economy'. Figures on the extent of this practice are difficult to obtain and no reliable estimates exist. 'Cohabitation' fraud refers to cases where people living with partners declare themselves as single when claiming assistance. A household in which a single parent lives with an undeclared partner on Social Assistance can thus receive 160 per cent (90 + 70) of the minimum wage rather than the 100 per cent paid to a couple (Table 4.2). Similarly, two adults each claiming to live independently receive a total of 140 per cent rather than the 120 per cent to which two adults sharing accommodation would be entitled. Again, there are no reliable estimates of the extent of this kind of fraud.

Two government Commissions were established in 1992 to investigate the causes and extent of fraud. Their findings highlighted the difficulties created by complexities of the Social Assistance scheme and the variability of local arrangements for scrutinising claims. Evidence on the extent of fraud was inconclusive. Although the Van Der Zwan Commission suggested that 25 per cent of all Social Assistance claimants acted fraudulently in some way, more recent information from the Central Bureau of Statistics shows that some form of fraud has been detected in only four per cent of all claims (evidence collected by Eardley *et al*, 1996).

In spite of the lack of firm data, fraud was believed by all study respondents to be a serious problem and policies to deal with it have been developed at both national and local levels. Locally for example, some municipalities carry out checks on 'black' fraud where unreported earnings are received from market stall selling or cab driving. In addition to regular checks on information supplied by applicants and claimants and the exchange of computerised information between authorities, severe penalties exist and prosecution procedures may be implemented if fraud is proved. The claimant is not usually prosecuted under criminal law, however, if the amount involved is small and if fraudulent claiming has lasted for only a few weeks. If overpayments are made they can be recovered from claimants or from other parties in certain circumstances.

Under the policy changes to be implemented in 1996, Social Assistance payments will be split into two parts - a national basic amount and a supplement granted by municipalities. The social minimum income will still be guaranteed by the legal responsibility of municipalities to grant supplements of up to 20 per cent but this maximum benefit will only be paid to claimants who can prove that they cannot share the cost of living with others. At present, the onus is on local authorities to prove that two people are not living independently. This shifting of the burden of proof will give municipalities more potential to develop local policies and practices for reducing fraud. There will be a financial incentive to do so since benefit supplements must be paid from a fixed block grant. Critics of government proposals to clamp down on fraud argue that this issue has been raised only in order to create a public climate of opinion favourable to cutbacks in benefits.

Policy implications

1996 changes and implications for local variation

Although the main element of Social Assistance remains at a nationally fixed level under the new scheme (which established the new general benefit, ABW), increased local discretionary powers could potentially lead to increased differences in total payment levels between municipalities. The basis for determining additional amounts to be awarded can vary between municipalities and during the negotiations leading up to the 1996 changes, the VNG (Union of Dutch Municipalities) presented four model options for consideration. The first was to relate each discretionary decision to the individual case, the second was to base decisions on broad categories of claimants and the remaining two options were combinations of these. Most municipalities are thought to be likely to choose the second option as being the easiest to implement. It will be possible to use central registration records to check the addresses of single people claiming to live alone.

There is evidence that some municipalities are sticking to previous rules while others are co-operating in designing new rules so that the same standards will apply in regional districts. Nevertheless, as one respondent pointed out 'not every local authority is capable of providing assistance in a correct, well-thought-out way'. Further monitoring of the implementation of the new legislation is required.

Advantages and disadvantages of the Dutch system

Equality before the law is seen as a major strength of Dutch Social Assistance. As a safety-net scheme, Social Assistance is seen as being relatively successful compared with other countries, offering a 'reasonable' level of benefit, at least in the first instance. Citizens can be certain of receiving a minimum income if in need. Relations between claimants and staff delivering benefits were described as 'very good', staff being 'really motivated to give a good service'.

One respondent saw the high cost of the scheme as a weak point and thought that levels of assistance should be related to people's 'real needs' rather than to minimum wage levels. Another, however, said that for people who remain on Social Assistance for two years or more, the levels of benefit were inadequate. The emphasis given to participation in the labour market is too strong, given the low labour market chances of many recipients. Complexity of the rules was also cited as a weakness, often exacerbated by differences between central and local government policies.

Chapter 4: ANNEX

Full names of benefits in Dutch

AAW	Algemene arbeidsongeschiktheidswet (General Disability Benefit)
ABW	Algemene bijstandwet (National Assistance Act: General Assistance)
AOW	Algemene ouderdomswet (General Old Age Pensions Act)
AWW	Algemene weduwen en wezenwet (General Widows and Orphans Act)
BB	Bijondere Bistand (Special Assistance)
BZ	Bijstandsbesluit zelfstandigen (Special provision for self-employed)
IAOW	Inkomensvoorziening oudere en gedeeltelijk arbeidsongeschikte werkloze werknemers (Act on Income Provisions for Older and Partially Disabled Workers)
IOAZ	Inkomensvoorziening oudere en gedeeltelijk arbeidsongeschikte gewezen zelfstandigen (Act on Income Provisions for Older and Partially Disabled Formerly Self-Employed)
RWW	Rijksgroepsregeling werkloze werknemers (General Unemployment Benefit)
TW	Toeslagenwet (Supplementary Benefit)
WAO	Wet op de arbeidsongeschiktheidsverzekering (Disablement Insurance Act)
WW	Werkloosheidswet (Unemployment Benefit)
WWV	Wet werkloosheidsvoorziening (Unemployment Benefit payable for one year)
ZW	Ziektewet (Sickness Benefit)

5 Sweden

Sweden is an exemplar of the so-called Nordic welfare state. With a population of 8.75 million (1994), it has a relatively high fertility rate of 2.0 in 1993. It has the lowest rate of marriage and a relatively high divorce rate. In 1993 just a half of all births were outside marriage, though many were to co-habiting couples. In 1990, 19 per cent of all families with children were headed by a lone parent, 16 per cent of whom were men.

For most of the post-war period Sweden has experienced high levels of employment, high levels of labour force participation and high levels of expenditure on social protection. However, economic problems over the past decade have resulted in an increase in unemployment from 1.9 per cent in 1987 to 8.3 per cent in 1992: economic participation remains the highest in the OECD at 80.7 per cent.

Although Sweden is now considered to be a leader in social security provision it was, in fact, a rather late starter. The general pension scheme was introduced in 1913 and this is at the heart of Swedish social security, having developed into a universal, non-contributory Citizen's Pension with an earnings-related second layer, which has contributed to a low rate of dependency on Social Assistance in old age.

In consequence Sweden has been characterised as having a residual system in terms of numbers dependent on benefit and its cost, relatively high benefit levels and replacement rates, a 'tough' means-test in terms of the treatment of income and assets, strong 'insertion' policies (work-test and training requirements) and a considerable degree of local discretion (Eardley et al, 1996). This chapter draws on, complements and up-dates that previous analysis of Swedish Social Assistance and in particular presents additional information on the issues of localisation and discretion.

Sweden's social (cash) assistance arrangements are determined by a single section of the Social Services Act 1980 where policy objectives are declared. Section 6 states:

-    The individual is entitled to assistance from the social welfare committee towards his livelihood and other aspects of living if his needs cannot be provided for in any other way.

-       The assistance must assure the individual of a reasonable level of living (Skälig). The assistance must be designed in such a way as to strengthen the independent living resources of the individual.

The social welfare committee is a committee of the municipality (though its name varies from place to place) and the Act gives broad responsibilities to the municipality for 'ensuring that persons....receive the support and assistance they need' (section 2), it must 'familiarise itself with living conditions in the municipality' (section 5), it 'shall take steps and ensure that steps are taken to create a social environment and good conditions for children and young persons, elderly persons and other groups in need of special support from the community. In the course of its activities the social welfare committee is to assert the right of the individual to employment, housing and education.' (section 9).

Other sections of the Act cover the social welfare committee's responsibilities to provide services for groups that in the UK are the responsibility of Social Services Departments, including people who abuse alcohol or drugs, children and young persons, elderly persons, people with handicaps, people needing residential care and so forth. Thus the provision of cash assistance is firmly embedded in locally administered personal caring services. Social cash assistance is estimated to take about one third of the staff resources of the municipalities' individual and family care services.

The vast bulk of the social security system in Sweden, both contributory and non contributory, is administered by central government agencies. Thus, in most municipalities there is a government office responsible for administering insurance benefits and another local office of the Ministry of Employment dealing with employment issues. However Social Assistance is the responsibility of the municipality.

There appear to be strong political, financial, administrative and cultural commitments to the municipality level administration of Social Assistance. If anything there has been a trend towards the deregulation of local government. The Local Government Act 1991 gave municipalities new freedom in structuring their committees and reforms in local government finance have increased their autonomy. The economic downturn of the early 1990s or 'The Crisis' as it is known in Sweden, has not led to any fundamental challenge to municipal control of Social Assistance. Local government is still (1994) responsible for spending 25 per cent of Sweden's GDP.

The national government (of whatever persuasion) support the present arrangements and the review of Social Assistance, presently under way, is merely seeking greater clarification and certainty about the respective roles of central and local authorities.

In terms of total GDP or total social security expenditure cash assistance is relatively insignificant (0.4 per cent of GDP and 6.7 per cent of social security expenditure in 1992). In 1993 it represented 4.3 per cent of the expenditure of municipalities but it has been increasing. Since the turn of the century until the late 1980s the proportion of the population receiving cash assistance at any one time fluctuated between four and six percent. The proportion of the population receiving cash assistance increased in the late 80s and early 1990s as a result of immigration and structural changes in the labour market. By 1994 eight per cent of the population were receiving cash assistance. Between 1980 and 1988 expenditure (in 1980 constant terms) on cash assistance increased from 1000 million SEK to 2000 SEK and by 1991 it had doubled again to 4000 million SEK.

Centre-local relations

Swedish public administration is organised in three tiers, each with their own political government (elected at the same time every four years) and their own powers to levy taxes.

At central level there is cabinet government and ministries. The latter includes the Ministry of Health and Social Affairs which is responsible for Social Assistance. It is rather small. State agencies play an important role and Social Assistance is the responsibility of the National Board of Health and Welfare.

Under the Ministry and Board there are County Administrative Boards covering 24 County Councils. County Councils are responsible for health but do not have much to do with Social Assistance.

The third tier consists of 288 municipalities who are among many other things responsible for Social Assistance. They vary greatly in size - about 50 per cent have fewer than 20,000 residents and a third of the population are in the three largest municipalities - Malmo, Gotteborg and Stockholm. The biggest municipalities have local district offices to administer Social Assistance.

Table 5.1

Tier	Number	Population
Level 1 (national)	1	8.75m
Level 2	24 County Councils	Varies
Level 3	288 Municipalities	50% have fewer than 20,000. 3m live in Malmo, Götteborg & Stockholm

The National Board for Health and Welfare has departments responsible for general policy, statistics (a responsibility taken over from Statistics Sweden in 1995), development and training, evaluation and special (big) projects. The Board acts in an advisory capacity only. Thus every five years (only) it publishes a 120 page booklet containing advice for municipalities on the administration of Social Assistance. The booklet contains advice on how to deal with each client group, each social circumstance, how family resources are to be treated, what claimants should be expected to do, what information should be made available and other relevant matters. In between the appearance of this booklet the Board distributes circulars. There appear to be four basic sources of authority for this guidance: the Act, proposals issued with the Act (which are considered by the Parliament but do not seem to have the authority of our Statutory Regulations), decisions of the Administrative Courts (see below) and the Board's own judgement.

The emphasis of all these arrangements is **guidance**. The decisions of the Administrative Courts and the advice of the Board may be influential but individual municipalities are free to interpret the Act in their own way. This independence is reflected in and is a function of the financial arrangements and, as will be reported later, there is evidence that this independence leads to considerable variation in the decisions made.

Finance and control

The cost of Social Assistance is born by municipalities who raise revenue to fund it by local income taxation. This is true subject to two reservations:

1.   About 25 per cent of the expenditure on Social Assistance nationally goes to refugees and the municipalities are refunded by central government for the first 3.5 years' costs (including Social Assistance) of a refugee's residence in their area- on a diminishing scale. However the refunds are not direct but distributed via a block grant.

2.   Local government finance is (inevitably) very complicated and changing with a new scheme, recently and painfully agreed, being implemented from January 1996. At present municipalities raise over 80 per cent of their own revenue, 55 per cent of this by income tax and the rest in user charges and other local sources.

There are two overriding principles governing central/local financial relationships. First there is a 'funding principle' whereby the state undertakes not to impose new obligations on municipalities unless they are prepared to fund them from central revenues (similarly if centrally administered responsibilities are withdrawn so will state revenues). Since 1993 there has been a move away from earmarked grants towards generalised funding and the new scheme gives even more discretion to municipalities to determine their own priorities.

Second there is the 'equalisation principle'. The latest version of this (starting in January 1996) involves:

1.   *Equalisation of taxation income* - which ensures that municipalities have a tax base corresponding to the national average. This involves redistribution between municipalities.

2.   *Equalisation of structurally related costs*. This is a needs-based redistribution - again between municipalities. The redistribution takes account of a list of activities (with Social Assistance subsumed under Individual and Family Care. This is the second largest activity after Care for the Elderly). Needs for each activity are represented by a number of indicators derived from regression analysis (with need for Individual and Family Care represented by the proportion of lone mothers, the proportion of migrants and non nordic nationals and population density).

3.   *A general per capita grant*. This is the only vehicle the state has for

controlling the costs of the local government sector. It is also the vehicle for compensating local government for new responsibilities.

4.   *Earmarked allowances*. For example the arrangements for refugees.

5.   *Transitional rules* - allow a phasing-in period of eight years to allow the municipalities who are big losers under the new scheme to adjust to the changes.

In 1995 386 billion SEK was spent by the local authorities and only 70 billion SEK came from central government sources. This proportion of 18 per cent is not expected to change under the new financial arrangements.

So control over the activities of municipalities is rather limited through financial mechanisms. It also appears to be limited in other ways. Thus there are no formal mechanisms for the central regulation of local expenditure, no rules governing the overall level of local taxation, no restrictions on local capital or revenue expenditure, no national local government audit or performance review, no central financial audit (this is left to the municipalities using private accountancy firms), no monitoring of financial performance, administrative efficiency, or indeed overall effectiveness. Municipalities do not have to balance their budgets, though they do have to have a three year financial plan and there are discussions taking place about the need for municipalities to balance income and expenditure. Parliament temporarily suspended municipalities rights to raise their tax rates in 1991, 1992 and 1993 but at present the municipalities regulate their own finances.

Norms

At the heart of current debates about the central/local relations in Social Assistance is the issue of the norms. In interpreting the Act the Board of Health and Welfare, despite the consistent opposition of the Association of Local Authorities (who see this as an assault on municipalities' freedom), has published cash assistance norms designed to provide a reasonable standard of living. The current ones are derived from the 1985 Budget Standard of the Swedish National Consumer Council. They set out the needs of a single person and couples and children, rather like the Income Support scales but broken down into a variety of commodities - food, clothes and shoes, leisure, personal care, cleaning materials, furniture, paper/phone, electricity, insurance, medical costs. In addition they list a number of items not included in the basic norms: rent, travel, child day-care, union dues and large medical expenses - these the municipality might consider helping with at their discretion.

The total sum represented by these norms was found to be above average of all OECD countries in 1992 (Eardley et al 1996). In cash terms the amount for a single person in 1995 was 3451 SEK (£345 per month in exchange rate terms), 5712 SEK for a couple and 1964 SEK for a child aged 4-10 (note however that in Sweden rent includes heating and normal rent is covered separately from cash assistance in housing benefit). The norms are detailed in Table 5.2.

Table 5.2   Swedish Cash Assistance Norms, 1995, SEK per month

	Single Person	Couple	Child aged 0-3	Child aged 4-10	Child aged 11-20
Food	1595	2868	824	1119	1315
Clothing & shoes	402	794	295	369	378
Leisure	187	378	98	173	238
Personal care	131	271	196	48	74
Household goods	116	164			
Furniture, tv, radio	417	541	220	220	220
Newspaper, phone, tv license	360	384			
Electricity	155	164			
Insurance	33	42			
Medical/dental charges	57	116	33	33	33
TOTAL	**3451**	**5712**	**1666**	**1964**	**2261**

Note: In addition housing (including heating) costs are added.   Also allowances may be made for essential transport.

Purchasing Power Parity: £1 sterling = 15.6 SEK in 1995
Exchange Rates: £1 sterling = 10.0 SEK in 1995

The National Board uprates the norms each year on January 1 and they have been adopted by an increasing proportion of municipalities. This trend to employ the norms was reinforced when in 1993 the Supreme Administrative Court ruled in two cases that the municipalities should in normal circumstances base their decision on the Board's guideline norm when judging what is a reasonable standard. There was also the hilarious case of a municipality which refused to accept the decision of a County Administrative Court that they were paying too little and bailiffs were ordered to seize goods from the municipality on behalf of the client in lieu of the short-fall. The councillors were subsequently fined for refusing to accept the Court's decision.

However more recently five factors have led to the norms coming under greater scrutiny which may eventually lead to the new Act introducing statutory national scales.

1.   'The crisis' led to increasing numbers of short-term recipients claiming Social Assistance. It has been argued that they do not need help with some of the items included in the norms - replacement/repairs of furniture, household utensils, TV, radio etc.

2.   The price index used to uprate the norms (and other benefits) has included housing. Housing costs have been rising faster than the costs of other commodities. Yet the normal housing costs of recipients of Social Assistance are covered by housing benefit separately from cash assistance. Thus the uprating formula has overestimated the actual increase in costs experienced by recipients.

3.   Real earnings have fallen (by 2 per cent between 1989 and 1993), taxes have increased as have charges for health care, housing and child care. Child benefits have been reduced (from 750 SEK to 640 SEK and the supplement for the third child abolished for new claimants) and insurance benefit as a proportion of previous earnings have been reduced from January 1 1996 (unemployment and sickness insurance benefits were cut from 80 per cent to 75 per cent of previous earnings).

4.   Both 2 and 3 have meant that the differentials between Social Assistance and income from either insurance benefits or earnings (known in Sweden as *respektavstand* - distance of respect) have

narrowed and are likely to narrow further. It is estimated that couples with two children on low earnings have experienced a fall of 10 per cent in real living standards between 1992 and 1995.

5.   Municipalities are anxious about increasing costs on their budgets. In addition the Swedish Association of Local Authorities has been irritated by the tendency of Administrative Courts to impose obligations of what they see as a political character on municipalities - 'The inclusion in framework legislation of a legal rights element to be implemented via administrative appeal constitutes a clear encroachment on local autonomy' (Riberdahl 1992, p10).

In addition to these factors, as a result of a decision by the Supreme Administrative Court in 1994, municipalities have been permitted to exclude household goods and other irregular expenditures when considering claims. About one third are now doing this.

As a result of all this, the new Social Welfare Bill was expected to include for the first time a framework of scale rates in a three tier structure - a rate to cover basic items (food, clothes/shoes, leisure, personal health, cleaning requirements, paper/phone/TV) which would be specified by the Act and uprated with inflation, an element to cover non basic items (furniture) which would be left to the discretion of the municipalities, perhaps guided by the Board and thirdly other payments for special items which would be left entirely to the discretion of municipalities (electricity, household insurance, medical and dental care). This scheme was proposed by a Parliamentary Commission on Social Assistance in 1993 and approved by the municipalities (subject to agreements over funding). However the incoming coalition government in September 1994 had reservations about appearing to cut benefit levels and delayed the Act. Now there is disagreement between the Minister of Social Affairs and the Minister of Finance about the level of the proposed basic statutory element (the Minister of Finance naturally wants it lower). With elections for a new party Chairman and Prime Minister in spring 1995 it is likely that legislation will be further delayed.

Perhaps, because of improving labour demand, the efforts already in place to enhance labour supply and the general pro-work perspective in the Swedish system, there is little evidence of deep concern over the issue of incentives. Nevertheless there is a view shared by both municipalities and central government that the norms are too high.

Coverage

Cash Social Assistance is available to anyone in need who meets the criteria of the municipality. In practice they must have income in a given month below a certain norm and be without any other resources. In the OECD study Sweden (Eardley et al., 1996) was found to have one of the toughest means-tests of any country in the study. There is no earnings disregard and all other income is fully taken into accounts. Cash savings and easily realisable assets must be used before a person is eligible. After a time on Social Assistance owners will be expected to realise the value of their property and a motor vehicle will be expected to disposed of unless it is essential for work. Municipalities have a responsibility to provide child-care for every child over 18 months but a lone parent who becomes unemployed will lose their child-care place after three months.

Eligibility is assessed and reassessed on a monthly basis. Applicants are expected to apply in writing and complete a standard form giving information about their income and assets. All new case are interviewed. Emergency support is usually available at least for families with children. Benefit is paid by cheque into the clients' bank account. The municipality has computer links with the local employment and insurance offices and requires to see pay slips. It can make contact with the automobile register to check vehicle ownership and the Local Living Register (every resident has to register where they are living) which enables them to check the household circumstances of the client. Processing new claims takes between three and four weeks (in Solna).

Social workers at municipal level work to the guidelines of their own social welfare committee. In one of the municipalities visited the committee met weekly and in the other monthly to consider difficult cases and make decisions. Each municipality has rules about what type of application needs to be referred to the Committee and in one of the municipalities the Committee considers four randomly selected cases at each meeting.

Cash assistance can be paid to complement low wages and about 20 per cent of recipients are working full-time for a the whole year. About one third of recipients get cash assistance as a supplement to unemployment benefit. Unemployed recipients who do not get unemployment benefit (about 15 per cent of the total) have either not been unemployed long enough to qualify for benefits (to qualify claimants must have paid unemployment insurance for 12 months and been employed for at least 80 days during the previous 365 days) or exhausted their entitlement to unemployment insurance (which lasts for 300 days except for the over 55 year olds, when it lasts for 450 days).

In 1994 63 per cent of recipient households were single people, mainly young. Couples with children were 15 per cent of recipient households and lone mothers another 15 per cent. In 1994 about 35 per cent of lone mothers, 16 per cent of single people, 2 percent of childless couples and 7 percent of couples with children received Social Assistance. In 1993 foreign born residents represented 10 per cent of the population, 25 per cent of Social Assistance recipient households and 50 per cent of the Social Assistance expenditure. Swedish households who form over 70 per cent of recipient households receive less than half of expenditure.

Most people receive Social Assistance for short periods. The average period was five months in 1994, 48 per cent received Social Assistance for less than three months while 18 per cent received it for 10-12 months. The latter cost half of all Social Assistance expenditure. In 1994 expenditure on Social Assistance was 10 billion SEK. This was an increase of 18 percent over 1993 (or 16 per cent in fixed prices).

Take-up is particularly difficult to define in relation to cash assistance in Sweden. There are substantial proportions of families with children with incomes
below the norms not receiving assistance. However some of these are ineligible because they have assets. Others would not be entitled because they or their partners are not willing or able to seek full-time work. The Health and Welfare Board estimated in 1994 that 15 per cent of households in the population had available annual income under the Social Assistance norms and only one fifth of these were receiving Social Assistance (National Board for Health and Welfare 1995).

Social Assistance and the local economy

The Swedish Welfare State is designed on the principle that everyone who can be, should be, in employment, full-time. Thus even lone mothers are expected to be in employment regardless of the age of their youngest child (after parental leave).

Policies to ensure high levels of labour demand and reduce unemployment have a central place in social (and economic) policy. If people are unemployed, sick or retired they will be covered by insurance benefits replacing substantial proportions of previous earnings. Cash Social Assistance has been for the very small minority who fall through this net. It was traditionally considered that those who needed Social Assistance for longer periods were people who had special needs in addition to the lack of work and income - needs that warranted the intervention of social workers - drugs, alcohol, behavioural problems, mental illness or handicap. Cash assistance was used as part of the armoury of social work to adjust their behaviour and where possible get them into work. Now the cash assistance system is having to deal with a much wider range of clients, more 'normal' people, for which by tradition and experience it was never designed.

Nevertheless there is great emphasis on getting recipients into jobs. Unemployed clients are required to register at the local labour exchange and may be required to demonstrate that they are actively seeking work themselves. In addition to the national job creation policies (which are considerable and involved 239,000 people in 1992, 5.4 per cent of the labour force) the municipalities can alone or in collaboration with the employment office establish their own work schemes. (Such relief jobs schemes had been established in both the municipalities visited.) Until recently there was an incentive to establish them. An unemployed person in such schemes for six months (or a year if newly employed) re-qualified for unemployment insurance for a further 300 days, thus relieving municipal costs. Some municipalities, particularly in the north of Sweden are known to 'manage' their unemployed in this way. This device for transferring costs to the insurance system has been stopped from January 1996 when work in municipal work schemes will not qualify clients for unemployment insurance.

Sensitivity to circumstances and geographical equity

Notwithstanding the recommended norms, there are still very substantial variations within and between municipalities in what amount of cash assistance clients receive. Two, as yet unpublished, studies provide evidence.

Byberg, working at the University of Stockholm, has sought to explain the variations in municipal expenditure on Social Assistance. Starting with eighty explanatory variables she found that the best model, containing seven variables, explained only 53 per cent of the variation between the expenditure of municipalities. She found that the municipalities stated policy on norms did not contribute to the explanation of variation . In fact policy on norms bore little or no relationship to the actual amounts received by clients. Thus those municipalities that claimed they stuck to the Board recommendations tended to pay lower or higher amounts and those that claimed to pay only the basic Board norm in practice paid amounts in excess of it. She examined in more detail the outlying municipalities - the ten municipalities most above and the ten most below the expenditure predicted by the model. The ten with higher expenditure than expected tended to blame it on factors outside their control. Those with lower expenditure than expected tended to credit it to their own internal management.

Further detailed work is being undertaken to seek to explain the position of a sub-sample of outliers. But the researchers have already noticed that some low municipalities have adopted the Uppsala model.

The Uppsala model is a management system first introduced in Uppsala by Eileen Ronnlund in the mid 1980s. Extra social workers are employed (average case load of 20 instead of the usual 80) and unemployed clients are required to demonstrate that they are extraordinarily active in seeking work - for example providing evidence that they have made up to 20 job applications per week. There are questions about whether this regime, which has been adopted in many municipalities, is actually successful in getting people into work or merely, by dispiriting clients, deters them from claiming cash assistance. The Board (*Pra Milton*) are undertaking an analysis of two districts in Uppsala - the one with the model and the other without in order to evaluate its impact. The results will be available soon.

The Board have also commissioned a study which draws on research by Terum (1986) in Norway, Huby and Dix (1992) in the UK and an earlier Swedish study by Gustafson (1993) and which seeks to examine the use of discretion by presenting 200 staff with six model (fictitious) cases on which to make decisions. The results show quite extraordinary variations both in judgements about eligibility and in the amounts awarded. Of the three more routine cases 97 per cent, 97 per cent and 95 per cent of social workers thought they were eligible but the amounts awarded varied from 250 SEK to 11,657 SEK per month, 1488 SEK to 7022 SEK per month and 839 SEK to 14,877 SEK per month in each case respectively. Among the more unusual cases 37 per cent of social workers thought that an old alcoholic normally on assistance, seeking extra money having lost his wallet was eligible and awards ranged from 334 SEK to 6,567 SEK per month. Only 41 per cent thought a young man who had left his job and gone on holiday and was coming back without any money was eligible and awards ranged from 350 SEK to 6667 SEK per month. Interestingly the more qualified social workers making judgement on the cases were less likely to decide the clients were eligible and more likely to award lower amounts. Younger social workers in some cases tended to award more to younger clients and older social workers more to older clients. Male social workers in some cases gave women clients more than women social workers. The judgements made on the same case showed great variation both within and between municipalities.

Bergmark (1987) has evaluated an experiment by a municipality *(Eskilstuna)* that tried to separate their administration into cases requiring the standard application of norms and those requiring special treatment. It proved very difficult to discriminate between the two groups and made no difference to the perception of clients about the way they had been treated.

While this evidence of inequity in the administration of Social Assistance in Sweden is a cause of concern in the Board and among some of those responsible for managing Social Assistance at a local level, it is not (yet) a public issue. No doubt this is because Social Assistance is still not a salient benefit and still seen as a locally and individually discretionary enterprise.

Stigma

There is still a good deal of stigma associated with applying for cash assistance. Social Assistance is one of the least popular income security systems in the Swedish Welfare State (Svallfors 1987). Though it has been suggested that some of the stigma of claiming is diminishing, particularly for younger people, this is not yet revealed in surveys of the client population.

A study by Hallerod (1995) asked a general sample their views about recipients of Social Assistance.

-       43 per cent did not agree with the statement 'Most people that receive Social Assistance do really need the support'.

-       70 per cent agreed with the statement 'Many of those entitled to Social Assistance do not apply'.

- 61 per cent agreed that 'Many of those receiving Social Assistance are *utslagna* (down and out)'.

- 58 per cent agreed that 'Many people receiving Social Assistance are cheaters'.

- 47 per cent agreed that 'Many recipients of Social Assistance are lazy and lack willpower'.

Bergmark (1996) believes that in the face of rising costs and expenditure there has been a growing tendency to blame Social Assistance recipients for ' general moral atrophy and too generous eligibility conditions'. He gives as an example a 1994 Department of Finance Report (*A Social Insurance*)which concentrates on the perceived negative incentive effects of current compensation levels and eligibility conditions. The report presents a *grunbults-teori* (keystone theory) - the Social Assistance scheme sets the keystone and that normal structures of reward are perverted if the last safety net does not keep undeserving applicants out, or allows compensation levels to overlap with earnings. These ideas are nourished by well publicised reports of single cases where social workers may well have been mistaken and clients may well have exploited the system. Such cases are treated as representative of general policy and result in calls for cuts in compensation levels, strengthening of eligibility standards and tougher controls. Bergmark argues that there is no evidence of widespread abuse of Social Assistance, that the measures proposed would not save a great deal of money and would result in eligible clients being made worse off. Furthermore there is no empirical evidence in support of the neo-liberal idea that Social Assistance is a keystone of the incentive structure.

Appeals and redress

Decisions made by social workers can be appealed by clients to the Committee, to the County Administrative Court, the Crown Administrative Court and to the Supreme Administrative Court. Only the Supreme Administrative Court sets legal precedent - decisions by the County and Crown Administrative Court only apply to the case being dealt with. There were no data on the numbers of appeals but the municipalities said that they were fairly common and the most usual reasons for appeal concerned the work requirements, the level of benefit, the rent limit, refusal to pay debts, the elderly relatives of refugees and the requirement to move to a less expensive dwelling. Appeals are dealt with only in writing and about 90 per cent were unsuccessful.

Conclusions

Although the salience of the Social Assistance scheme has been increasing in recent years it still plays only a residual role in the overall social security scheme. Nevertheless it is the focus of a good deal of attention at present and at the time of writing the outcome of a review of the system by central government has not been resolved. The review was established as a result of the tensions created for a highly residual scheme with (in British terms) a considerable degree of local discretion being subjected to pressure from the downturn in the Swedish economy. These pressures have led to tensions between central and local government over the financing of the scheme, to disputes between municipalities and the administrative courts about the status of the guidance they are given by the National Board for Health and Welfare and a debate about whether the norms recommended are too generous. The debate continues.

Meanwhile there is evidence emerging from research studies that there is very considerable variation in the treatment of like cases both within and between municipalities. However, this does not seem at present to create any great concern about equity. This is perhaps because the scheme is still highly residual and because cash assistance is still seen as part of the armoury of the social work service. In that context, it is recognised that variation in decision making is an inevitable consequence of flexible individualised discretion.

What are the advantages and disadvantages of the Swedish scheme? Clearly there is room for argument about merits and defects depending on the perspective from which one comes.

Among the advantages of the scheme the following may be identified:

*   the level of the benefits paid which are comparatively generous.
*   the emphasis on 'insertion' and more specifically the efforts made to encourage and enable claimants to re-enter the labour market and

undertake training. Services to support that objective, for example child care are in place.

* in that context the fact that the scheme is administered at municipal level with a good deal of freedom to take account of local circumstances is an asset.

* the staff administering the scheme are qualified social workers subject to close political supervision - thus it is both a highly professional and democratically run service.

Among the disadvantages of the scheme that may be identified:

* there is no doubt that there is still a considerable amount of stigma associated with receiving Social Assistance and partly as a result of this there is evidence that many of those eligible fail to claim their entitlement.

* the means-test and behavioural requirements are comparatively tough (at least in comparison with British experience). The process of claiming may be very intrusive.

* local discretion enables municipalities to pay benefits below (and above) the norms recommended and to impose (or fail to impose) requirements on claimants that national policy makers may not consider desirable.

* the norms may be too high and overlap too much with income from work i.e. replacement rates are too high.

* there are tensions between central and local government over the issue of norms and these have been complicated by decisions of the administrative courts.

* these tensions are associated with disputes about responsibility for funding the scheme - though central/local fiscal arrangements seem to have been settled for time-being.

* perhaps the most striking characteristic of the Swedish scheme is the very considerable amount of variation in the treatment of like cases. This of course can be viewed as gross inequity - the scheme is a lottery and what you get depends too much on where you live and who you see. On the other hand it may be viewed as one of the benefits of flexible, individualised discretion.

6 Switzerland

A small and independent country with a population of just under 7 million in January 1994, Switzerland has a high proportion of foreign workers (about 14 per cent of the population in 1992) and a birth rate just above the average for the European Economic Area. It has a relatively young population and a support ratio which is lower than the average for OECD countries.

Although, in exchange rate terms, Switzerland has the highest income per head of all OECD countries, and traditionally has experienced both low inflation and low unemployment, it has recently shared in the problems of the wider international economy. From a very low base unemployment has increased to 3.7 per cent compared to an OECD average of 7.8 per cent. Recent economic and demographic changes have resulted in a dramatic increase in claims on social aid but it remains a marginal element in an insurance based programme.

Table 6.1   Number of authorities by tier in Switzerland

Tier	Number	Population Range
Level 1 Federal	1	6.9 million
Level 2 Cantons	26	14,000 to 1.14 million
Level 3 Communes	c3000	24 to 500,000

Switzerland is a federation of 26 cantons. The canton is the key constitutional unit. Powers can be transferred from the cantons to the federal government only where there is express legislative provision and only after elaborate processes of consultation and, often, a referendum. Within the cantons, the many communes do not have formal constitutional status but their powers, duties and obligations are set out in canton law. Within the boundaries defined by canton law, the communes are autonomous. There are elected bodies at each level (commune, canton, federation). Communes have representatives on canton parliaments; cantons elect representatives to the federal parliament.

The principle of subsidiarity has traditionally applied and continues to do so. The principle and practice of local decision making are very strong and are widely defended. As in other federal structures, there is a certain scepticism and distrust about the role of the federal administration in the constituent states (Bendix, 1992).

There is an equally strong tradition of direct democracy which, in addition to voting for representatives at commune, canton or federal level includes the frequent use of the referendum and of the formal provision for 'initiatives' whereby the competent authority is required to respond formally to any petition which commands a certain minimum support (Kriesi et al, 1992). Extensive consultation forms a part of policy development though this does not appear to have much formal structure. There are two national standing 'conferences' in the social security field - the *Konferenz der kantonalen Fürsorgedirektoren/Conference des Directeurs Cantoneaux des Affaires Sociales* (CDAS) is a conference of ministers in canton governments; the *Schweizerische Konferenz für öffentliche Fürsorge/Conference Suisse des Institutions d'Assistance Publique* (SköF/CSIAP) is the conference of officials in canton and commune administrations. Both exercise a consultative and co-ordination role and have clear interest in harmonisation and *SKöF/CSIAP* publishes annually guidelines for the calculation of Social Assistance. However, neither conference has any executive role in the development of policy.

Switzerland therefore displays a very powerful pluralist tradition which inhibits any concentration of power and generally tends to favour gradualist approaches to change in policies or structures.

Policy objectives

Nobody in Switzerland discusses Social Assistance solely in terms of the usual working definition - 'the range of benefits and services available to guarantee a minimum (however defined) level of subsistence to people in need, based on a test of resources' (Eardley et al, 1996, p xiii). Arrangements for Social Assistance, thus defined, are an integral part of, and inseparable from, a broader concept of social aid which has been described in terms of three concentric circles. The inner circle is *personal aid* - information, advice, counselling on a personal and individual basis from, usually, a social worker or other professional. *Social Assistance* in the form of payments in cash or in kind and based on a test of resources is the second circle. A range of *health, social, educational and employment services* comprises the outer circle.

The explicit objective of social aid is to achieve the reintegration of people in need so that they maintain or recover social and economic independence. Financial support is not just about ensuring survival but is also about encouraging the client to play an active role in society (see, for example, Fribourg 1994; Geneva, 1996). So, the outcome of the consultation between the client and the social worker is expected to be a package of actions which might include financial assistance but would also include, for example, job search, education, training or any other positive action on the part of the client which will advance the objective of reintegration. This package is frequently described as a contract between the individual and the community of which he/she is a member.

Social aid is conceived as a very residual safety net provision to deal with clients who do not derive adequate assistance from the social insurance schemes. There are separate and very comprehensive insurance schemes for retirement pensions, survivors' pensions, unemployment benefit, occupational accidents and disease pension and sickness and invalidity benefits. Provision for these is made in federal law, though they are administered by a variety of public and private agencies. The retirement, invalidity and survivors schemes cover all persons domiciled in Switzerland or engaged in paid employment in Switzerland or Swiss citizens working abroad for a Swiss employer.

In addition, there are the second and third 'pillars' of insurance - compulsory occupational provision and voluntary private provision. Social insurance represented 69 per cent of the total 'social budget' in 1990; private insurance was 9.6 per cent, Social Assistance was 2.4 per cent.

Social Assistance can interact with insurance in three ways :

- Social Assistance can be paid as a bridging arrangement until insurance payments start;
- Social Assistance can be paid as a supplement to insurance benefits where the latter are insufficient to support the household. There are formal arrangements for 'complementary pensions' which are paid in

addition to retirement pensions and guarantee an income equivalent to the minimum insurance benefit payable with a complete insurance record;

- Social Assistance can be paid when entitlement to insurance benefits has expired.

Recent economic and demographic changes have resulted in a dramatic increase in claims on social aid. The number of persons assisted has at least doubled in the period 1990 to 1995 (Tschümperlin, 1994 and later estimates). Nevertheless, it remains a residual element in an insurance based programme. An estimate of 250,000 persons assisted in 1995 represents about 3.6 per cent of the population of 6.9 million.

In the field of social security, the federal government is responsible for social insurance. Social Assistance is explicitly the responsibility of the cantons. With very limited exceptions, the federal parliament and government have no responsibility for policy, finance, the levels of benefit or administration. The exceptions are:

- a federal law which determines which canton is responsible for the support of which people in a set of rules largely based on domicile though the original canton of residence is responsible for the first two years after an individual has moved to another canton.
- the federal government provides financial support for Social Assistance to asylum seekers (about 17,000 per annum in recent years having been much higher earlier).
- the federal government is responsible for payments to Swiss citizens abroad.

There are some moves towards greater harmonisation and a degree of greater centralisation in the determination of the levels of benefit payable within Social Assistance.

The lower house of the federal parliament has drawn up a Bill to provide for the setting of some minimum guaranteed level of support in federal legislation though this Bill provides for a number of alternative approaches to this. The Bill is a response to a federal court judgement that there is an implicit right in the federal constitution to a minimum level of existence and the subsequent calls for this to be enshrined formally in the constitution and also to other concerns that there should be some minimum standard in financial terms below which no individual should fall. The decision on whether or not a right to a minimum standard is inserted in the federal constitution and, if so, what form it should take will depend largely on the attitudes of the cantons. The Bill is currently out to consultation. The process will probably take two years to complete. The proposal is controversial and the outcome is unpredictable. It is certain that the cantons will resist the setting of minimum standards in explicit financial terms if the cantons are to remain responsible for raising and disbursing the finance.

Centre-local relationships

Given the extremely limited role of the federal government, the crucial relationships are those between the canton and its communes. This relationship varies between cantons and emerges from negotiation between the parties. Communes can and do raise petitions against the canton government. The relationship is also intimately connected with the system of financing.

In the cantons visited, the following patterns of relationship in the administration of social aid were observed:

A: Policy and administration centralised at canton level but administration distributed in the communes and co-located with other health and welfare services (Geneva)

This unique example of centralised services is an historical accident rather than a deliberate decision but is acceptable to all the parties. There have been no objections from the communes. Locating professional staff in local offices enables local residents to get to know their own workers and provides the opportunity for collaborative working with other health and welfare professionals. However, this arrangement does mean that professional staff are spread rather thinly and places a high premium on the quality of communication from the centralised headquarters, especially when changes in policy are to be notified. Information technology was shortly to be introduced in an effort to improve communications. Inter-professional working cannot be mandated. Whether it happens in a given locality depends on the attitude and goodwill of the individuals concerned.

B: **Professional social work services provided by the canton; Social Assistance provided by the communes** (Graubünden)

This arrangement is designed to ensure that clients in small communes have access to advice etc. from professionals despite the commune's inability (or possibly unwillingness) to finance the services themselves. It also protects the client from the exercise of arbitrary power by the commune authorities by providing an objective, third party source of advice and, if necessary, advocacy. The package deal for each client is, therefore, negotiated between the social worker and the commune authorities.

C: **Services provided by the communes but subject to close supervision by the canton** (Basel-Land)

This arrangement is intended to provide some professional oversight of local decisions to ensure that they have been taken in accordance with canton guidelines and advice. Every decision is monitored before implementation. The arrangement is not uncontroversial. There has recently been a petition by the communes against the canton arguing that the canton was exercising too much power and seeking a redistribution in favour of the communes. The canton's response leaves social aid as a commune responsibility. Some intended relaxation of the supervisory role is as much a response to the pressures of rising numbers as to the communes' demands for more autonomy.

D: **Services in the process of being provided by 'regions' comprising several communes rather than by the communes as previously** (Vaud)

As with Graubünden, this policy is designed to ensure access to professional services for all clients. The initiative came from the canton and, after much discussion, a pilot project in four regions has commanded support. Subject to the outcome of consultation, currently in progress, the structure will be extended to the whole canton by 2000. The new structure improves the quality of professional services. It increases clients' access costs to a degree although the new regions are still quite small geographical areas and travelling distances are not great. The cost implications are, at best, neutral. The economies of scale, if they exist at all, are modest: the substitution of salaried professional social workers for elected, voluntary members of local commissions increases costs.

E: Services provided by the communes (Bern and Zürich)

The canton authorities are involved in the promulgation of advice (e.g. the *SKöF/CSIAP* guidelines) persuasion and discussion but do not have executive functions.   Where the canton has significant responsibilities for funding (e.g. in Zürich), this can create a situation of responsibility without power for the canton.

Financial

In principle, the authority responsible for making the decisions is responsible for raising the revenue to fulfil those decisions. The strict application of the principle of subsidiarity would impose these costs on the communes. This has caused some problems for the small communes arising from a number of factors, viz.:

- rising number of applications for Social Assistance;
- increasing numbers of individual cases with a high cost (such as alcohol dependency or a lone parent family with several children and non-payment of maintenance);
- longer duration on Social Assistance associated with the increased difficulty of successful reinsertion which accompanies higher unemployment;
- the prohibitive cost of employing professional staff from a small budget;
- the rapid increase in the costs of some items which Social Assistance payments must cover, especially housing and health insurance.

In practice, therefore, the principle has been widely modified by the use of various cost-sharing schemes. These take different forms in different cantons but are all designed to ensure that all clients in need can have their needs met even if the client is a member of a small community or of a comparatively poor community or of a community which is experiencing unusually high demands on its services.

The arrangements consist of:

- the creation of a 'pool' to which both the canton and the communes contribute.
- the creation at canton level of a special fund to finance especially difficult or expensive individual cases (e.g. drug or alcohol abuse) so that these expenses do not represent an unreasonable burden for a small commune budget.
- redistribution between communes but with no involvement of canton funds sometimes involving all the communes, sometimes involving only the poorer/smaller communes leaving the big communes to be self sufficient.

The capacity of the communes to contribute to these schemes is calculated on the basis of taxable base and (usually) population and (sometimes) volume of other obligations such as education or so as to place a ceiling on the amount of tax raised in the commune for social purposes. These can involve complex formulae which are recalculated each year.

None of the budgets is cash-limited. Cantons and communes each have powers to raise taxes and they usually employ income and/or wealth taxes for most purposes. If a budget proves insufficient to meet demands, the shortfall must be met by increasing taxation (which all cantons and communes are seeking to avoid), transfers from other budgets (which are difficult to achieve) or borrowing (which thus becomes the usual method of financing deficits). Pressure on budgets is greatest in the cities. Budgets have so far proved adequate in many places.

To the extent that the cost sharing or other arrangements separate decision making which commits resources from the responsibility to generate those resources, moral hazard is created. There is a real incentive for communes to seek ways of transferring costs to other budgets e.g. by strict application of the domicile rules, by seeking out unclaimed insurance benefits, or by having recourse to canton special funds. For example, the canton of Basel-Land created a special canton fund for particularly expensive cases (especially drug or alcohol rehabilitation) in 1990. Claims on this fund quintupled by 1994 before levelling out. Some of this increase can be attributed to meeting previously unmet need but not this rapid escalation.

Coverage

The social aid schemes are intended to cover any persons resident in Switzerland who are unable to support themselves and their families by their own efforts. Within this broad and inclusive definition there is no further specification of client group or of any policy priorities or targets though some canton documents give *examples* of groups whom the canton has a duty to assist (e.g. Bern, 1993)

Whether financial assistance will actually be granted depends on:

- a detailed assessment of the client's overall needs (financial and non-financial) and of the client's own resources and capabilities;
- the willingness of the client to comply with the provisions of the package deal which emerges from the assessment of need;
- the application of the principle of subsidiarity.

Social Assistance and the local economy

Since the express aim of Social Assistance is to promote social and economic (re)integration, there is an intimate link to the local economy in the packages of financial and practical assistance which are formulated. There is a general expectation that clients will work if they possibly can and they are therefore expected to seek work. The exceptions are lone parents of very small children who have no access to child care and disabled people whose disability is sufficiently serious to prevent their doing any sort of work. In an economy with traditionally low levels of unemployment, finding work has been a realistic expectation for most people. And one of the advantages claimed for local administration is the knowledge of where jobs exist in the locality.

The canton of Geneva has recently (effective from 1 January 1995) introduced a new scheme for unemployed people whose entitlements to unemployment insurance are exhausted. This establishes for the first time an entitlement to a legally mandated minimum payment of Social Assistance but also establishes an obligation to perform 'compensatory activity which has social or environmental value'. The same legislation creates access to a grant of up to SFr 10,000 for re-training, setting up a business or 'professional or social re-integration'. The 'compensatory activity' seems largely to consist of tasks which would normally fall to volunteers (e.g. shopping, gardening or decorating for the elderly or housebound people). The distorting effects are, therefore, felt in the voluntary sector rather than in the formal labour market.

Geneva's law is unusual in creating formal rights and obligations. It is generally seen, however, as a natural progression from existing practice rather than a significant change in policy direction.

In all cantons visited, the package of aid includes measures to improve the client's employability where this is felt to be necessary (e.g. assessment and/or training programmes) and financial assistance can be dependent on participation in such schemes.

With the recent rise in unemployment, formal demand management measures are becoming more general. These include job creation schemes and other schemes in the second or parallel economy which require socially useful activity of clients and provide the disciplines of a workplace and which provide sheltered workshops for people with disability. Unofficial demand management seems to have been a feature of many schemes throughout. In country areas dependent on forestry or agriculture there are always jobs that need doing (albeit seasonal and short-term) and the local network will match the client to an activity.

The level of financial assistance is intended to facilitate active participation in normal social life. It is explicitly not a subsistence scheme.

Sensitivity to circumstances

The essential *raison d'être* of the Swiss Social Assistance schemes is that decisions should be founded on a detailed evaluation of the particular circumstances.

SköF/CSIAP publishes detailed guidelines on recommended levels of financial assistance which recognise a wide variety of family forms and possible expenses. A summary of the main recommendations is at Annex A. Guidelines issued by the cantons to commune authorities may elaborate on these recommendations and list other expenses which can be covered by Social Assistance (a list giving examples of such additions is at Annex B). *SKöF/CSIAP* guidelines suggest capital limits and canton guidance may identify a wide variety of resources which should be taken into account - income, capital and (in some cases) livestock. The suggested capital limits appear low by British standards (see Annex A, section [L]).

The unit of evaluation is those people in a household who share resources. Although the constitution states that parents have a duty to assist children and *vice versa* and the principle of subsidiarity identifies the extended family as the point of first resort, in practice people outside the immediate household are not usually asked to provide assistance. The exceptions are absent parents who are in default of court-ordered child or spousal maintenance, who will be pursued quite aggressively, and where it is obvious that the relatives are well-off. Where there are people who do not form part of the claim, but who do live in the same house as the client, they will be expected to contribute a proportionate share of common expenses such as lighting costs.

Decisions are made after close examination of the individual circumstances and the pattern of costs and income. Clients are required to provide evidence of their circumstances and Social Assistance authorities are empowered to make enquiries of third parties. In many cantons, tax returns are still public documents and can be examined.

In principle, every decision is individual but the *SKöF/CSIAP* guidelines are increasingly accepted as norms. They are becoming more widely known, not just to Social Assistance authorities but also to the general public. Though the Social Assistance authorities themselves do not publicise them, the guidelines are generally available for purchase and popular magazines such as *Der Beobachter* carry articles about Social Assistance as well as other advice to people in need.

The Social Assistance awarded will be lower than the guidelines figures if the client's normal level of income was previously lower than the guideline figure. There have been suggestions that lower sums were also paid if the commune was under financial pressure or if the guideline figure was deemed by the decision maker to be high in relation to his/her (the decision maker's) own financial circumstances. These two reasons are regarded as illegitimate and the pooling of resources and the professionalisation of services are intended to mitigate any such tendency.

Nevertheless, the *CSIAP/SKöF* guidelines are not a rigid tariff. They contain a number of optional features and some of these are expressed as ranges rather than as a single figure.

Housing costs are usually met in full after account is taken of any possible contribution from other members of the household. There is some discretion to pay less if the accommodation is reckoned to be excessive for the household's needs. Geneva has formal financial ceilings for the contribution to housing costs. These are felt to be reasonable for single people and couples as small apartments are fairly generally available. It is felt to be rather strict on families with children as larger apartments are both scarce and expensive. Vaud has indicative ceilings but with some flexibility to vary them in certain circumstances.

Some cantons systematically deviate from the guidelines. Geneva consistently produces its own guidelines which set the level of general support 15-20 per cent higher than the *SköF/CSIAP* guidelines. Partly, this reflects the higher cost of living; partly it is a reflection of a particular philosophy in that canton. Aargau has recently issued guidelines which are intended to reduce costs by 10 per cent as a response to economic pressure. This is controversial and is helping to fuel demands that some minimum figure should be formally established in federal law.

If the client fails to comply with other conditions in the package (such as training), the financial assistance can be reduced. In practice, it appears that this discretion to reduce payments is exercised only in relation to 'extras' such as pocket money and not to those elements which constitute essential expenditure.

Clients must report changes in circumstances but, in any case, regular review by the social worker would be likely to reveal any significant changes. All cantons/communes provide for a formal review at least annually. Some require a fresh application every 12 months. More frequent reviews may be programmed depending on the circumstances. In some problematic cases, there may be weekly meetings. There are no limits on how long assistance can continue. In principle, Social Assistance payments are repayable and this principle is restated in canton documents. In practice, repayment is sought only in exceptional circumstances such as inheritance or winning the lottery. A client who receives a normal salary would not be regarded as being in circumstances which permitted repayment.

Geographical equity

There is widespread variation between and within localities. The justification for this is that each package of assistance must be tailored to the individual circumstances though there would appear to be much bunching around the norm. This variation is not controversial. Switzerland tolerates, even celebrates, diversity.

There is a civil rights issue which relates to the way in which some guarantee of existence can or should be expressed in constitutional terms.

Stigma/peer pressure

In the centres of population, which have long had professional services, this is a general issue. There is a generalised stigma in a country which has little unemployment and a strong work ethic against those who do not work when they are capable of doing so but this is lessening as the experience of unemployment becomes more general.

In the small communes it raises very specific issues of concern. There is agreement that the process of submitting to a detailed examination of one's personal and financial circumstances by members of the Social Assistance commission who are also one's neighbours and colleagues in other community activities has a serious deterrent effect. The decision making by elected representatives rather than professional social workers personalises the process to an unacceptable degree. The maintenance of client confidentiality becomes virtually impossible. The number of cases in any one year may be so few that they can, in effect, be identified from the published accounts and annual report. At worst, the attitude of the local decision makers can become seriously judgmental and the client can be victimised or rejected. These are not marginal concerns. Twenty eight per cent of the population lives in communes with fewer than 5000 inhabitants and no professional services (Fragnière, 1994). Some communes are very small indeed with only hundreds or, even, dozens of inhabitants. The various measures to provide professional services in all localities, however small, are attempts to prevent these outcomes and to provide objectivity and privacy for the client.

There is very little evidence of client attitudes. One survey in Geneva suggested that, even in a centralised and professionalised service, the clients felt the process of investigation was oppressive and made them feel guilty.

Appeal mechanisms

Rights of appeal vary between cantons. In principle, the appeal is to the proper authority with responsibility for social aid, that is, the commune or canton representatives as the case may be. There is come provision for an administrative review first and for a final appeal to a legal commission. Historically, these provisions were little used but are becoming more so as the concept of rights gathers support and as the financial norms become more widely known, The little detailed evidence available - from one canton only - nevertheless, suggests that only about 2-3 per cent of cases produce appeals and about half of these are making specific claims to particular payments - e.g. to run a car or for reimbursement of the costs of dental treatment. Few appeals succeed.

Take-up of benefits

Take-up is a difficult concept to apply when there are no entitlements. Evidence which compares applications for Social Assistance with the numbers of people with incomes below certain commonly used poverty definitions suggest *de facto* take-up is very low indeed. In country areas, take-up may be as low as 20 per cent. Research in the city of Bern, which has a population of 130,000, estimated that in 1991 (i.e. before the recent increase in unemployment) 17.2 per cent of adults had a monthly income of SFr 1000 or less. This compares to *SKöF/CSIAP* guideline income of SFr 970 for a single person, not including housing costs. Yet, less than 4 per cent of the Bern population were receiving Social Assistance - a very crude take-up rate of about 24 per cent. (Bern, City of, 1992) Similar ratios appear in the parallel study of the canton of Bern (Bern, Canton of, 1992). Earlier studies, variously conducted between 1976 and 1990, produced a wide range of estimates of people in poverty from 4.4 per cent to 23.3 per cent. Lone parent families and single men all represented disproportionately among the low income group.

Simplicity

These schemes are not simple. Transaction costs for the client are high in terms of time and effort and psychologically. With no rules of entitlement, it is difficult for clients to form a view in advance about whether the effort of application is worthwhile.

Estimates of administrative costs are few and unreliable. It is plain that a scheme of this kind is labour and skill intensive relying as it does on individualised enquiry, interview and supervision by professionals. Figures from one canton show salary costs as 21.4 per cent of the social aid budget in 1994 with professional staff comprising 70 per cent of that total.   This intensive use of professional staff is acknowledged by officials in Social Assistance authorities even if they have no detailed figures for administrative costs. The costs are seen, however, as a price worth paying. The social aid schemes in their entirety are regarded as a necessary investment in human capital which pays dividends in earlier and more effective return to valuable economic activity and the prevention of individual alienation and social fracture.

Control of fraud

Fraud is not an issue. It is acknowledged that there is some degree of misrepresentation of circumstances but the extent is estimated as very small and any active measures to counteract it as counterproductive. Wide ranging or systematic fraud would be difficult to achieve. Clients have to produce detailed evidence about their circumstances which can be checked. Domicile and taxable income are a matter of the public record. The black economy is small. There has been some intensification of the initial checking of statements in some places but, beyond that, increased effort is not seen to be justified.

Pressure points

The issue which is dominating discussion is the increase in unemployment. Though this is still low by international standards at four per cent, this is historically high for Switzerland and is as high as seven per cent in some cantons. The reasons for this increase are identified as structural and, therefore, unemployment is expected to remain at high levels for some extended period albeit at levels a little below the current ones.

Unemployment is contributing to the increased demands on Social Assistance in two ways - more claims and longer duration of claim. About one third of unemployed people have been unemployed for longer than one year. The response is to intensify labour market efforts both on the supply side in training and education and on the demand side by job creation. The major concern is about clients with limited ranges of skill for whom job opportunities are becoming increasingly limited and for whom there is a risk of very long term unemployment.

The impact of other demographic change is discussed but does not have anything like the same prominence. It is commonly believed that families are voluntarily continuing to provide substantial amounts of help, both practical and financial, to family members in need. So, if people nevertheless seek Social Assistance this is because the family's capacity to continue to help has been overstretched. The consequences of marriage breakdown are the most obvious signs of family stress with large proportions of separated or divorced women needing help from Social Assistance at some point soon after break-up. The divorce rate is commonly quoted as 30 per cent

According to demographic forecasts, Switzerland will have a fairly large increase in the proportion of retired people. This is not, apparently, a pressure point. The officials who provided us with information have little direct experience of services for elderly people as these are normally separately administered. But the main reason for the lack of concern is that the three pillars of the retirement insurance scheme - compulsory state insurance, compulsory occupational insurance and voluntary private insurance - will be sufficient to maintain standards of living for the retired population. The comparatively small numbers of elderly people who receive Social Assistance would suggest that confidence in the robustness of the retirement insurance schemes is not misplaced but the low take-up figures may disguise unmet need.

The big unknown is the extent to which lessening stigma, greater public knowledge of guideline figures, the higher profile of the civil rights debate culminating, possibly, in constitutional change may stimulate demand and generate much higher take-up.

Summary

Consistent with the principle of subsidiarity and with the long tradition of local administration, the Swiss systems of Social Assistance display much variety in their organisational forms and in their financial arrangements. Most are also in the process of some adaptation in response to changing circumstances whether these arise from changes in the external environment (e.g. rising unemployment) or from internal policy initiatives (e.g. to enhance professional standards). Nevertheless, there are some common themes which were present in all, or most of, the cantons visited.

Advantages of the Swiss approach to Social Assistance

-       financial support is part of an integrated package of practical and personal support and assistance. All respondents reaffirmed the objective of achieving social and economic integration and autonomy for the persons in need and were convinced that this integrated and personalised approach was the most effective way of achieving this key objective. Financial support was not to be regarded as separate from other forms of help.
-       local decision making meant that decisions were made by persons familiar with the social and economic circumstances of the locality as well as with the personal circumstances of the individual. Thus, decisions would be well-informed, practical and feasible. Indeed, the familiarity with the local circumstances can promote imaginative and creative solutions and encourage offers of practical help.
-       local supervision facilitates easy monitoring of the individual's progress with the agreed plan.
-       the idea of a contract between the individual and the Social Assistance authorities promotes and strengthens community solidarity especially the notion of mutual rights and obligations.
-       a community's elected representatives are close to, and thus fully aware of, the reality of the social and economic situation in the community and of the pressures placed on the community's resources and on those of individual households.

Disadvantages of the Swiss approach to Social Assistance

-       in small communities, local decision making is effectively decision making by one's neighbours. The necessary enquiries are intrusive and confidentiality can be seriously compromised.
-       the requirement to provide details of personal circumstances and finances to other members of a small community can have a significant deterrent effect. In consequence, the proportion of people receiving

financial assistance is low compared to estimates of people on incomes low enough to be able to derive benefit.

-   decision making is often by elected representatives (the Social Assistance Commission) of the community and not by professional staff. Decisions can be influenced by personal considerations (e.g. the decision maker's own income) and not by the merits of the case.
-   it is possible, and has been known, for families to be rejected by a community and to be denied assistance.
-   individual cases which merit high volumes of support (e.g. people suffering from drug or alcohol abuse needing rehabilitation; large families not receiving child maintenance) can have a devastating effect on the tax burden of a small community.
-   financial systems can become very complex. There is a real incentive to attempt to shift financial responsibility to another budget and some of the structures create moral hazard.
-   there are few, if any, formal rights to assistance and few efforts by the authorities themselves to publicise arrangements.

Conclusion

The Swiss systems of Social Assistance are deeply embedded in the political, social and cultural traditions of the country. The structures have been created from the bottom up and the principle and practice of subsidiarity actively govern the way in which the systems operate and the questions relating to those systems are addressed. There is still powerful support for the concept of local decision making and the flexibility and creativity which that approach produces. Though the disadvantages of the approach are acknowledged (and measures to ameliorate them are being implemented in some places), the advantages are perceived to be much greater.

The challenges to the approach come from two main sources - the developing demand for explicit rights to a minimum level of existence and economic pressures.

The issue of how the right to a minimum existence is to be guaranteed is controversial though the principle itself is not. It has already been declared by the courts that there is an implicit constitutional principle. The cantons and communes would strenuously resist the federal mandate about the actual minimum level of payment but there would be less resistance to a statement of principle and some description of the nature of the support to be provided. The resistance to a legally mandated minimum reflects the strength of support for a system which can reflect local circumstances. It also reflects an equally strong feeling that if the cantons and/or communes are to foot the bill then they must be free to make the decisions. Finally, it reflects a traditional distrust of any centralising tendency.

In practice, however, there have been pragmatic moves towards a voluntary harmonisation of financial norms. The *SKöF/CSIAP* guidelines remain guidelines but they have steadily achieved a salience which means that, with rare exceptions, they are used as norms and there is deviation from the recommendations only where special circumstances dictate. The salience has been achieved by greater recognition of the advantages of harmonisation by the Social Assistance authorities and because the guidelines are better known among the general public who can therefore use them as a benchmark. The major motivation for harmonisation is to protect the value of the suggested awards and to prevent a reduction in their real value.

The economic pressures arise from increasing numbers of unemployed people whose entitlement to insurance benefits has expired, from longer duration on Social Assistance benefit and from increasing numbers of individual cases that incur high costs. In all instances, these phenomena have a low incidence by international standards but they are at historically high levels by Swiss standards and, as such, are a cause for concern. The response has been to make more strenuous efforts to reinsert people into economic activity, job creation and the creation of socially useful activity in the 'second' or 'parallel' economy. Significant elements in the *SKöF/CSIAP* guidelines have not been increased in value for four years and so there has been some reduction in the real value of the suggested awards. Apart from that, there has been little pressure to reduce benefit levels or to reduce access to benefit and what pressure there has been has been successfully resisted. The controversial exception is the canton of Aargau which has proposed guidelines 10 per cent below the *SKöF/CSIAP* ones. The justification for the maintenance of both benefit levels and social work activity is that the overall objective of a return to economic and social independence is best served by early investment in the people; that any reduction in that investment would be counter-productive in that it would delay successful reinsertion and so risk the individual's becoming detached from economic and social activity altogether. There is knowledge of the discussion in Britain and the USA about the underclass. There is no evidence in Switzerland of discouraged workers losing contact with mainstream society and the Social Assistance authorities are determined to prevent any such tendency. In their view, greater rather than less initial activity and preservation of a normal lifestyle is the best way to achieve this. The situation is worst in the cities where the increasing numbers of claimants and the reluctance to raise taxes has resulted in budget deficits. This cannot continue but, for the time being, the pressure to reduce costs is mainly being directed at other services.

The changes that have been, or are being, made in the systems are addressing some of the disadvantages of localised decision making. The major issue concerns professionalising decision making and so avoiding the problems of decisions based on inadequate assessment of the individual's circumstances or other considerations which are personal to the decision maker. The greater use of professional social workers introduces an objectivity into the assessment and provides the claimant with a protection against the exercise of arbitrary power. The big communes have long had professional services. These standards are being extended to the smaller ones, which cannot afford to recruit social workers of their own, by regionalisation (as in Vaud) or by provision by the canton of social work service (as in Graubünden) or by the pooling of costs (as in Bern).

Stigma is undeniably a feature of the Swiss approach though, it is suggested, this is lessened as the number of successful applicants increases and dependence on Social Assistance becomes less remarkable and as the concept of rights gathers support.

The Swiss approach, which features both localisation and discretion in large measure, has remained robust and widely supported despite recent economic and social change. It is being adjusted in an essentially pragmatic way and the general expectation is that this process of gradual adaptation will continue. This approach may not be sustainable if the economic situation worsens and/or if the low levels of take up were to increase dramatically in the wake of reducing stigma and more overt statements of rights. Though these are possible developments, there is nothing to suggest that they are probable, at least in the short to medium term.

Annex A

CSIAP/SKöF GUIDELINES FOR THE CALCULATION OF Social Assistance, 1996 SFr AND £ PURCHASING POWER PARITY

(a)   Maintenance

Household size	maintenance per person per month		maintenance per household per month	
	Sfr	£	Sfr	£
1 person	670	190	670	190
2 person	500	143	1,000	285
3 person	420	120	1,260	359
4 person	370	105	1,480	422
5 person	340	97	1,700	484
6 person	320	91	1,920	547
7 person	305	87	2,135	608
8 person	293	84	2,344	668
9 person	283	81	2,547	726
10 person	275	78	2,750	784

Expenditure on clothes, shoes and laundry for children up to 11 years and for baby products is included in these amounts.

(b)   Pocket money

for young people from 12 - 16 years old	SFr30-60	£8.5-£17
for each person of 17 or older	SFr150	£43

(c) **Charges for radio/tv/telephone including proportion of taxes**

for single person household   SFr70-90   £20-£26

for households with 2 or more people   SFr80-100   £23-£28

(d) **Clothes, shoes, laundry**

for young people from 12-16 years old   SFr60-80   £17-£23

for each person of 17 or older   SFr80-100   £23-£28

(e) **Cost of meals taken away from the home**

20 main meals   SFr185-230 £53-£65

(f) **General work costs**

in full-time work   SFr200-250 £57-£71

(g) **Extra assistance**

For unemployed people who perform well in
work experience or substitute work programmes   SFr200-250 £57-£71
analogous with (f) above for people in work

(h) **Capital limits (one-off)**

for one person   SFr4,000*   £1,140*
for a couple   SFr8,000*   £2,279*
addition for minors   SFr2,000*   £570*

*doubled if there is no possibility of building new assets in the future

Annex B

Expenses which might be covered by social assistance payments

The following is a list of items which are mentioned in canton guidance. Their inclusion here is intended to give a view of the scope envisaged for the Social Assistance schemes. There is no guarantee that the expenses would always be met.

gas, electricity, heating if not included in rent

up to three months arrears in rent in certain circumstances

furniture and furniture maintenance

insurance for house contents and third party liability

removal expenses

sickness and accident insurance

up to six months arrears on sickness and accident insurance

retirement insurance

medical expenses

pharmaceutical expenses

dental charges

travelling expenses (but not usually the use of a private car)

child care expenses

7 Conclusions

Although each of the countries included in this study was included because they exhibit varying degrees of localisation and discretion in the development, financing and delivery of social assistance they are, in fact, quite dissimilar in most respects. A previous study of social assistance (Eardley et al 1996a) assigned each of the four countries to a different social assistance regime.

Taking into account a range of indicators (which in addition to the central/local dimension in regulation and administration included: total extent, cost and coverage of social assistance; relative level of benefit provided; the operation of the means test and the degree of officer discretion) it was concluded that Germany had most in common with Britain, Canada and Ireland; they were typical of welfare states with integrated safety nets. Switzerland, however, was linked with Austria in their exceptionally high degree of decentralisation and local discretion. The Netherlands, like Luxembourg, Belgium and France, provide a dual system of support: categorical assistance for specific categories of claimant now supplemented by relatively new, general, basic safety nets. Finally, Sweden was classed as being an exemplar of residual social assistance schemes of the Scandinavian variety. Here social assistance has, until recently, played a marginal role in social security and society.

That each of these countries has, in the final analysis, more in common with third party countries than with each other, underlines a critical conclusion from this study. To focus on one or two dimensions (localisation and discretion) without regard to either other aspects of social assistance policy and administration or to the wider socio-political context, is to risk an unbalanced perspective. Much can be learnt from studying the development and implementation of social assistance policy in a national context. There are clear limits, however, to the extent to which patterns of convergence can be observed and examples of 'good practice' identified with a view to their adaptation/application in another context.

Nevertheless, the study has confirmed the importance of analysing arrangements for the administration and financing of Social Assistance in a double context:

First, in each of the four countries Social Assistance has to be considered as part of wider social security provision. In each country Social Assistance has played and continues to play a subordinate role in income maintenance when compared to social insurance and minimum wage provisions. In 1992, for example, whereas 33 per cent of the UK's social security expenditure was committed to Social Assistance, the proportions in Germany, the Netherlands, Sweden and Switzerland were, respectively, 12 per cent, 11 per cent, 7 per cent and 1.8 per cent. In addition, the proportion of national populations in receipt of Social Assistance, despite having increased in all countries, were significantly lower in the countries under review than in the UK. For example, in 1992, 15.3 per cent of the UK population were receiving Social Assistance; in Germany, the Netherlands, Switzerland and Sweden the proportions were, respectively, 6.8 per cent, 4 per cent, 6,8 per cent and 2.3 per cent.

Second, the policy making, administrative, financial and accounting arrangements for Social Assistance are, in large measure, determined by the prevailing traditions of governance in each country. The existence and authority of national constitutions, formal structures to represent different tiers of government and political values which simultaneously bind nations together while acknowledging the diversity of sub-national experience all contribute to the configuration of unique polities. A detailed examination of structures for the administration of Social Assistance necessarily elide into wider considerations of national political economy.

In Germany, responsibility for Social Assistance is shared between three tiers of government. At the Federal level, which is responsible for policy making, regulations are derived from the Basis Law, the Federal *Sozialhilfe* Act (BSHG) and the Social Code. At a regional level, the *Länder* meet on a formal basis to exchange information and to set the levels of benefit. Local authorities are responsible for 80 per cent of financing of Social Assistance and administer the scheme.

Although there is scope for variation between local authorities this is now minimal with respect to the basic scale rates and the trend is for the differences to narrow even further. However, there are differences in the structures and vitality of local economies and these contribute to variation in rates of dependency and to unevenness in the levels of one-off payments. The Federal government has proposed legislation which seeks to diminish variations in the value of these discretionary payments which have been a major cause of appeals. Overall, and despite the importance of local authorities in financing and administering the scheme, the structure and 'tone' is top-down, reflecting the dominance of Federal interests and policy agendas.

Social Assistance in the Netherlands is also regulated by national legislation but administered by municipalities. The scheme is financed through general taxation and rates of benefit are fixed nationally in relation to the minimum wage. Historically, there is no local discretion in respect of either condition of eligibility or basic scale rates. However, growth in the cost of Social Assistance and in the numbers dependent on benefit stimulated new legislation which was implemented in January 1996. There has been a move towards more effective targeting of benefits and a campaign against fraudulent claims. This is to be achieved by adjusting Social Assistance payment to local circumstances: the basic amount payable to a single person is reduced to 50 per cent of the minimum wage and the basic amount payable to a lone parent reduced from 90 per cent to 70 per cent/ However, the trend towards the additional devolution of financial responsibility and discretion to municipalities has been accompanied by the application of increased constraints on municipal budgets and the guidelines within which they must operate. It is too soon to assess the new scheme in practice.

In Sweden, in contrast to the majority of social security (which is administered by central government agencies) Social Assistance is the responsibility of municipalities. There is a three tier structure to governance: at a national level there are a number of ministries, including the Ministry of Health and Social Affairs which, via the National Board of Health and Welfare, have ultimate responsibility for Social Assistance. Although the 24 County Councils have responsibility for health they have no remit for Social Assistance, which is the responsibility of the 288 municipalities.

The National Board for Health and Welfare provides advice and guidance to the municipalities, covering such topics as the treatment of resources in the assessment of benefit and the rights/obligations of claimants. This guidance may be influential but individual municipalities are free to interpret the national Social Services Act (1980), where policy objectives for Social Assistance are stipulated, in their own way. Social Assistance is funded by the municipalities out of local income taxation and there is a considerable degree of independence from national/central control. The National Board of Health and Welfare publish cash assistance norms which are designed to provide a reasonable standard of living. Traditionally these have been adopted and implemented by municipalities but a growth in the number of short term Social Assistance claimants together with concern about the impact on the budget of local authorities has resulted in a position where approximately one third of municipalities now make payments having excluded certain items from the list of 'norms'. There is a broad and growing consensus between central government and municipalities that the cash assistance norms are too high. There is also (limited) evidence of significant variations in the treatment of similar cases between municipalities.

The downturn in the Swedish economy has contributed to growing tension between central and local government over the financing of Social Assistance and there have also been disputes between municipalities and the administrative courts about the status of guidance given by the National Board of Health and Welfare.

Switzerland is a federation of 26 cantons - the key political and constitutional unit - which, in turn are composed of approximately 3,000 communes. There is a tradition of direct democracy and a firm commitment to pluralism which abhors the concentration of power.

Social Assistance, for the Swiss, exists between an inner circle of *personal aid* and a wider net of *health, social, educational and employment services*. The fundamental objective of Swiss Social Assistance is to facilitate the social and economic independence of recipients. To this end, financial assistance is complemented by a package of personal and practical support tailored to the circumstanced of individual applicants. The highly localised structures of policy making and administration affords opportunity for decisions to be made by individuals who are directly familiar with both the local environment and the needs to the applicant. However, this proximity and familiarity can have a negative impact on the take-up of Social Assistance.

Swiss Social Assistance, although highly diverse and localised, is not fully insulated from wider trends and pressures. On the one hand there is a growing demand for the specification of minimum standards of benefit and other, possibly contradictory, pressures associated with deteriorating economic circumstances. There have been gradual moves towards the voluntary harmonisation of financial norms across the cantons: a trend encouraged by Social Assistance authorities and supported by the general public. It is ironic that is precisely these tendencies which are contributing to a reduction in the salience of stigma as an aspect of Social Assistance provision and to an increase in the professionalism of decision making and administration.

Across the four countries, certain common (or similar) trends and experiences can be adduced. No country has been immune from the social consequences of economic change and recession. Whereas each of the countries under review has, until the late 1980s, maintained a national economy committed to low inflation and low unemployment, they have more recently witnessed a growth in numbers receiving Social Assistance. Increasing numbers of claimants have exhausted their entitlement to social insurance benefits and become (especially in the Netherlands and Germany) long term dependents on assistance. National governments, across a range of public sector programmes, have sought to contain the growth in, or reduce the levels of, expenditure. In each country there is growing concern with programme costs, fraud and negative behavioural implications which may contribute to benefit dependency, low motivation to seek employment or contribute to family break-down. There is, however, relatively little robust evidence to substantiate these concerns. New responsibilities have been assigned to private and non-for-profit sectors and there has been a tendency for functions (and accountability) to be devolved to subordinate authorities. At the same time, there has been encouragement for local authorities themselves to exercise financial restraint while coming under pressure from national authorities to, in the field of Social Assistance, increase job search conditions, refine eligibility criteria and promote new employment opportunities.

It is difficult to be precise about the implications, strengths and weaknesses of existing (and, in the case of the Netherlands and Sweden brand new) arrangements for the administration of Social Assistance. In Germany, Sweden and Switzerland there are, however, examples of moral hazard such that sponsored job opportunities for Social Assistance claimants are negotiated for one year only - just long enough to re-establish entitlements to continuing financial support from social insurance funds.

Although the capacity exists in each of these countries to vary the conditions of eligibility and the levels of payment, in practice there is much less structured adjustment to prevailing local circumstances than might have been anticipated. In Germany, for example, the indications are that variation in the cost of living is as great (if not greater) between urban and rural locations within a local authority than it is between authorities. In the Netherlands, and before the new scheme was introduced in January 1996, there was little variation in conditions of eligibility or basic scale rates. There is evidence, especially in Sweden and the Netherlands, of significant variation (more accurately inequity) in response to examples of urgent and exceptional need. This particularly relates to the exercise of officer discretion in relation to individual applications: experimental research has indicated that the same cases will be treated in different ways by different officers such that variation is related less to local circumstances than to the vagaries of individual decision making.

A major challenge for a review of this kind is the absence of much information which would be taken for granted in a British context. None of the countries has detailed information on the numbers and outcomes of appeals against administrative decisions. Similarly, there is a marked absence of detailed statistical information about the composition of the claimant population or the duration of claims over time. Partly because most locally organised and delivered schemes will have both cash and social work elements, and partly because practices of public sector accounting do not require it, there is an absence of robust data on the administrative costs of organising and delivering Social Assistance at sub-national levels. The presumption, in each country, is that the administrative (transaction) costs are relatively high, certainly higher on a case/unit basis than in the UK. Moreover, even where the concept of take-up is understood, there are no comprehensive or official data (in any of the countries) to estimate the levels of take-up and non take-up. Similarly, there are few reliable data on the extent or form of fraud in relation to Social Assistance.

In Social Assistance schemes, existing as back-up to social insurance and minimum wage regulation, where there are twin objectives for policy (relieving financial hardship to a prescribed minimum and promoting social integration to relieve exclusion) and where the numbers in receipt of benefit and the duration of claim are limited, then advantages associated with locally administered schemes are apparent. There is 'soft' evidence from each of the countries that the principle of localisation is appreciated and, indeed, valued. However, equally, as numbers in receipt of benefit have increased and resources have been contained, there is growing concern about moral hazard, the operation of stigma and the costs of administration. In Germany there is claimant resentment at both the degree of means-testing and the requirement that relatives are liable for maintenance. Stigma associated with claiming Social Assistance is reported to be especially high in Sweden and many eligible claimants do not apply. Take-up rates are adversely affected by the intrusive nature of the means-test and the expectations of high levels of behavioural conformity.

The strengths of these schemes, all manifesting a degree of localisation, are to be understood against a wider canvas which presents Social Assistance as a residual component of a larger and more inclusive structure of social protection, with strong traditions of social insurance and, until recently. low levels of unemployment. The displacement costs associated with the re-structuring of social insurance, demographic and family change and incased unemployment are placing strain on the traditional advantaged of locally based Social Assistance schemes: locally provided schemes appear to work best when the demands made upon them are manageable. As the scale of reliance on Social Assistance increases, so the advantages associated with economy scale derived from centralised administration, are better appreciated.

References

Allum, P. (1995) *State and Society in Western Europe* (Cambridge:Polity Press)

Bendix, Regina (1992) 'National Sentiment in the Enactment and Discourse of Swiss Political Ritual' *American Ethnologist* 19(4) pp. 768-790.

Bergmark, A. (1996) Individual morality and incentive structures - a problem for the Swedish Social Assistance Scheme? in Hamalainene, J. and Vornan, R (eds), *Social Work and Social Security in a Changing Society*, forthcoming.

Bergmark, A. (1987) *Only Money*, Social Work Report 38, University of Stockholm.

Bern, Canton of (1992) Direction de l'Hygiène Publique et des Oeuvres Sociales *La Pauvreté dans le Canton de Berne* Bern.

Bern, City of (1992) Fürsorge- und Gesundheitsdirektion der Stadt Bern *Neue Armut in der Stadt Bern* Bern.

BSHG (1994) *Bundessozialhilfegesetz*, 23rd edition, Kleinere Schriften des Deutschen Vereins für öffentliche und private Fürsorge, Eignverlag, Frankfurt.

Butcher, H., Glen, A., Henderson, P., Smith, J. (1993) (eds.) *Community and Public Policy* (London:Pluto).

Cawson, A. and Saunders, P. (1983) 'Corporatism, Competitive Politics and Class Struggle' in King, R. (ed.) *Capital and Politics* (London:RKP).

Cloasen, J. and Freeman, R. (1994) *Social Policy in Germany*. (Hemel Hempstead: Harvester Wheatsheaf).

CBS (1993) *Statistics of Public Assistance 1990-1991*, Netherlands: Central Bureau of Statistics.

Deutscher Bundestag (1995) *Gesetzentwurf der Bundesregierung. Entwurf eines Gesetzes zur Reform des Sozialhilferechts*, (Drucksache 13/2440), Bonn.

Eardley, T., Bradshaw, J., Ditch, J., Gough, I. & Whiteford, P. (1996a) *Social Assistance Schemes in OECD Countries: Synthesis Report*, Department of Social Policy, Research Report No. 46, HMSO, London.

Eardley, T., Bradshaw, J., Ditch, J., Gough, I. & Whiteford, P. (1996b) *Social Assistance in OECD Countries: Country Reports*, Department of Social Security, Research Report No. 47, HMSO, London.

Fintel, M. von and Wagner, E. (1989) 'Individueller Leistungsmißbrauch in der Sozialhilfe', in *Nachrichtendienst des Deutschen Vereins für öffentliche und private Fürsorge*, 1, 69, pp. 17-22.

Fragnière, Jean-Pierre (1992) 'Où va l'aide sociale?' in Fragnière, J-P; Sommer H G and Wagner, A eds. *Sozialhilfe/Aide Sociale* Lausanne, Direction du PNR 29.

Fribourg, Canton of (1994) *Loi sur l'Aide Sociale du 14 Novembre 1992: Aide-Mémoire à l'intention des services sociaux régionaux et professionels* Fribourg.

Geneva, Republic and Canton of (Département de l'Action Sociale et de la Santé) (1996) *Directives cantonales en matière de prestations d'assistance* Geneva.

Gustafsson, B., Hyden, L-C., och Salonen,T (1993) Decision-making on Social Assistance in Major Cities in Sweden, *Scandanavian Journal of Social Welfare*. 1993-2, sid. 197-203.

Hartmann, H. (1985) 'Armut trotz Sozialhilfe. Zur Nichtinanspruchnahme von Sozialhilfe in der Bundesrepublik', in Leibfried, S. and Tennstedt, F. (eds) *Politik der Armut und Die Spaltung des Sozialstaats*, edition Suhrkamp, Frankfurt.

Hollis, G., Davies, H. and Plokker, K. (1994) *Local Government Finance: An Internaitonal Comparative Study* (York: JRF).

Huby, M. and Dix, G. (1992) *Evaluating the Social Fund*, Department of Social Security Research Report No. 9, HMSO.

Hyden, L-C, Westermark, P.K. and Stenberg, S-A, (1995) *Att besluta om socialbidrag: En studie i 11 kommuner*, Centrum for utvardering av socialt arbete, Stockholm, Socialstyrelsen.

Jakobs, H. (1995) *Evaluierung von Maßnahmen der 'Hilfe zur Arbeit' in Bremen*, Centre of Social Policy Research, University of Bremen.

Kemperman, M. (1994) *The Provisions Guaranteeing Minimum Resources in the Netherlands*, Tilburg University: IVA Institute for Social Research & Department of Social Security Studies.

Kriesi, Hanspeter., Koopmans, Ruud., Duyvendak, Jan Willem and Giugni, Marco G (1992) 'New Social Movements and Political Opportunities in Western Europe' *European Journal of Political Research* 22, pp.219-244.

Leibfried, S., Leisering, L. et al. (1995) *Zeit der Armut. Lebensläuge im Sozialstaat*, edition Suhrkamp, Frankfurt.

Ludwig, M., Leisering, L. and Buhr, P. (1995) 'Armut verstehen. Betrachtungen vor dem Hintergrund der Bremer Langzeitstudie' in *Aus Politik und Zeitgeschichte*, B31-32, July, pp.24-34.

National Board for Health and Welfare (1992) *Social Assistance: General Advice from the National Board*, Socialstyrelsen.

National Board for Health and Welfare (1995) *Social Assistance - its recipients and development*, Socialstyrelesen 4.

Oorschot, W. van & Smolenaars, E. (1993) *Local Income Assistance Policies: the Dutch Case and a European Impression*, Tilburg: Work and Organisation Research Centre Paper 93.07.011/2B.

Oorschot, W. van (1995) *Realizing Rights: a multi-level approach to the non-take-up of means-tested benefits*, Aldershot: Avebury.

Riberdahl, C. (1992) *Have Local Authorities Come of Age? Address to the 3rd Seminar of the Nordic Conference of Local Authorities*, Swedish Association of Local Authorities.

Schulz, A. (1979) *Local Politics and Nation-States* (Oxford:Clio Press)

Spicker, P. (1991) *The principle of subsidiarity and the social policy of the European Community* in Journal of European Social Policy, 1,1, pp3-14.

Sozialhilferichtlinien (1995) *Sozialhilferichtlinien. Richtlinien und Anhaltspunkte zur Andwendung des Bundessozialhilfegesetzes*, second edition, Landkreistag Baden-Württemberg, Richard Boorberg Verlag, Stuttgart.

Svallfors, S. (1989) *Who loves the Welfare State*, Arkiv, Lund.

Terum, L.I. (1986) *Geografisk ulikskap og nasjonale normer. Variasjoner i behandlingen av socialhjelpsklientar.* Oslo, Institutt for anvendt sosialvitenskaplig forskning. INAS-rapport 1986-2.

Tschümperlin, Peter (1994) *Estimates of the Development of Social Assistance 1990-1994* Bern, SKöF/CSIAP.

Appendix

EVALUATION CRITERIA AND QUESTIONS

Context

The key characteristics of the Social Assistance scheme: its aims, objectives, legislative basis, role in relations to other parts of social security system. What are the traditions of centre-local authority (and politics) in each country? Are there trends towards more centralisation or more localisation? How accessible to potential claimants is the Social Assistance scheme?

Centre-local relationships

-       constitutional provisions: policy, powers and finance

-       is there variation, and in what ways, between theory and practice?

-       describe the principal lines of accountability and responsibility

-       to what extent can subordinate authorities influence higher bodies?

-       how are funds raised and allocated?

Financial

Who make the decisions and is responsible for the following:

-       what proportion of funding (of Social Assistance) is allocated to each tier of government?

-       how are these decisions taken? What is their rationale? Who makes the decisions?

- on what basis are sums of money allocated to localities?

- what are the costs of administration?

- what is the source and nature of funding? How is revenue raised?

- what happens if/when local (subordinate) authorities overspend?

- what controls and checks exist to ensure that expenditure is within limits?

- who checks and controls expenditure?

- are there audit checks? If so, by whom are they conducted?

Coverage

- what is the scope of the scheme? Who is deemed to be eligible? What is the rationale for their support?

- are the main recipients the intended targets of support?

- what action is taken (and by whom) to ensure that aims/targeting is achieved?

- to what extent is there local flexibility as to coverage/priorities/variation among groups of claimants?

Social Assistance and the local economy

- to what extent is the aim to link to local circumstances: local economy, labour market or housing market? This might include avoidance of disincentives/or creating incentives. Do schemes vary according to size of locality?

- how much discretion is there at a local level? Can benefit rules be wavered or altered in general or in relation to specific client groups?

- are there any specific measures to stimulate the local labour market? If so what are they? These might include job creation or training schemes.

- where schemes of this kind exist what evidence exists about their strengths and weaknesses? How is the monitoring and evaluation conducted?

Sensitivity to circumstances

- is provision made for recognition of different family circumstances?

- how much central guidance is there about flexibility in relation to flexibility? How is the guidance expressed and communicated?

- how are decisions about flexibility reached?

- what happens when claimant circumstances change? How often are claims re-assessed?

- is anyone (ever) left without assistance?

Geographical equity

- what evidence is there of differences in law, custom and practice in the treatment of claimants or setting of benefit levels by locality?

- what is the rationale for these differences?

- are any of the observed (or perceived) differences a source controversy? If so, why?

Stigma/peer pressure

- is there any evidence that local decision making encourages/discourages/requires stigma or peer pressure?

- if the pressure to exert stigma/peer pressure exists, is this the result of policy objectives?

- is there evidence of impact of stigma/peer pressure on the take-up of benefits, the duration of claim or behavioural change?

- is the scheme seen to be fair and without discrimination? Do views on this differ between officials (at different grades and locations) and claimants?

- are there any claimant satisfaction surveys? How are claimant views sought or known?

- are there rights of appeal? How are these exercised? Are they exercised? Is there any evidence about numbers, reasons and outcomes?

- is there anything similar to the British welfare rights lobby? In other words, are there local advice agencies? If yes, how are they funded and what do they do? Do they have a lobbying role? What are there campaign aims? How effective are they?

Simplicity

- to what extent does localisation/discretion promote systems which are simple, easy to understand and cost-effective to administer?

Control of fraud

- are there definitions of fraud? Are there estimates of the extent of fraud? How is fraud monitored and at what level? Are examples of good/bad practice identified?

-       are there local anti-fraud campaigns? How are these organised?

-       is fraud believed to be a problem?

Pressure points and policy options

-       what are perceived to be strengths and weaknesses of scheme?

-       where are pressures and difficulties experienced? How are these observed?

-       what proposals are there for change or adaptation?

-       are changes proposed for either aims or objectives?

-       what are the timescales for these changes?